Animation by FILMATION

compiled and written by
Michael Swanigan
and
Darrell McNeil

edited by
John Reed
and
Joshua Lou Friedman

ANIMATION BY FILMATION
by Michael Swanigan and Darrell McNeil
Copyright © 1993 by Michael Swanigan
All rights reserved. No part of this publication may be reproduced or used in any form or by any means— graphic, electronic, or mechanical, including photocopying recording, taping or information storage and retrieval systems — without written permission of the publisher.

Published by:
Black Bear Press
2828 Cochran St.
Suite # 152
Simi Valley, CA 93065

Printed and bound in the United States of America

Cover, Book Design and Layout by:
Michael Swanigan

Cover Characters:© ARCHIE COMICS, ©D C COMICS, WARNER BROS. ©KING FEATURES SYN., ©MATTEL INC., ©FILMATION, ©SHERWOOD SCHWARTZ, ©JERRY LEWIS

All artwork and photos used in this book are from the collections of the authors and are © copyrighted by the respective studios. No attempt is supercede the copyrights by their respective studios.

Dedications...

I am dedicating this book to Betty Hilliard (1918 - 1992) a woman, a mother, my grandmother, and my friend who made a big huge difference in my life, who help raise and mold me as a child. I will never forget "Life is what you make it, - so make it fun!" Dear, I know you can hear me, you are missed.

Always in my thoughts,
Michael Swanigan
1980-89 Storyboard Staff

I dedicate our book to a pair of good people, now no longer with us, who helped shape and influence my life in general and my Filmation career in particular:
to Wes "Pappy" Herschensohn, a billiant layout artist, and my first Filmation roomie, who took a nervous rookie layout artist and through his guidance, helped me achieve one of my first career goals: my first screen credit at age of 21...
and my dearly departed grandmother and best friend, Rosella J. Forrest, who didn't know a Riverdale High from Hero High, and didn't care, long as she knew that her grandson was a involved in making them happen.
Finally, a special tip of the "Big 'D'" topper to Bill Danch, Paul Fennell, and the 1977-78 Filmation Layout Bullpen ... you know who you are.
All gone ... and all much missed.

Darrell McNeil
1978-81 Layout Staff

Copyright © 2013 Black Bear Press

All rights reserved.

ISBN-13:978-1481225045
ISBN-10:1481225049

CONTENTS

INTRODUCTION 5
BY FONDER AND PRESIDENT LOU SCHEIMER

ANIMATION BY FILMATION 11

LIVE-ACTION BY FILMATION 135

STORYBOARDS BY FILMATION 149

HISTORY OF FILMATION 175

JOURNEY BACK TO OZ — © 1975 FILMATION • STAR TREK — © 1975 FILMATION — NORWAY PRODUCTIONS • ARCHIE — © 1968 THE ARCHIE COMPANY • TOM AND JERRY — © COPYRIGHT 1980 METRO-GOLDWYN-MAYER, INC. MIGHTY MOUSE — © 1980 VIACOM INTERNATIONAL, INC. • THE LONE RANGER — © COPYRIGHT 1980 LONE RANGER TELEVISION, INC • FAT ALBERT — © COPYRIGHT 1980 WILLIAM H. COSBY, JR. — FILMATION ASSOCIATES

INTRODUCTION

FILMATION
From "A" (Archie) to "Z" (Zorro)

FILMATION - a name that conjures various different meanings depending on the person it's directed to. To its admirers, it conjures up memories of an animation company that produced a large and diverse body of series and feature work during its 24-year existence (1964-1989). It was during that time, with only one exception, that the company managed to keep all facets of production in the United States. This fact is admirable in that every other American animation productions house sent the majority of its animation work overseas. Filmation also eschewed the violent content of its competitors in favor of a pro-social approach in its later productions.

To its detractors, Filmation conjures memories of an animation company which continually reused its animation throughout its series to save money and keep the work here in the states.

To a generation of baby boomers, it conjures up memories of an animation company that entertained them with favorite characters from TV, movies, comic books, and children's literature brought to colorful (and sometimes "tuneful"), animated (and live-action) life.

To Michael Swanigan and Darrel McNeil, it conjures up memories of some of our childhood's favorite series (with Darrel, **The Archies**, **The Hardy Boys**, and **The Batman/Superman Hour**; with Michael's, **Fantastic Voyage**, **Groovie Goolies**, and **Jerry Lewis**) as well as a studio where they both spent time working on a variety of series. Some of the shows they worked on were variations of the ones they watched as youngsters.

And for those of you who bought this book because the name "Filmation" on the cover made you think to yourself, "Hey, didn't they make...?" Well, between the letters "A" (Archie) to "Z" (Zorro), you should find something within these pages to magically conjure those memories bursting forth from the dark recesses of the "child" part of your mind...if it ever *left*, that is!

by Lou Scheimer

Lou Scheimer

Founder and President, Filmation Associates

A BRIEF HISTORY OF FILMATION

THE EARLY YEARS

In 1962, a young animation artist named Lou Scheimer founded Filmation, a company destined to become one of America's premiere animation studios.

At first, the studio produced commercials and documentaries. Then, in 1965, Filmation unveiled its first Saturday morning series, **Superman**. It was an instant hit and ran for three years on CBS. *Superman* was followed by several other successful series, bringing some of the world's best-loved comic book heroes to life. By the late 60's Filmation had produced **Aquaman**, **Batman**, and the phenomenally rated **Archies**.

In the 1970's, Filmation continued to produce new animated series for all three networks, including programs such as **Groovie Goolies, The Brady Kids, Mission Magic, Jerry Lewis, The Fabulous Funnies, Mighty Mouse, Heckle and Jeckle, Lassie, Space Sentinels, Gilligan's Island** and **Gilligan's Planet**.

INTO THE 80's

Filmation dominated the fantasy and adventure fields. Following in the footsteps of its earlier classics **Fantastic Voyage** and **Journey to the Center of the Earth**, the studio went on to produce **Tarzan, Zorro, The Lone Ranger**, a full-length **Flash Gordon**, and the Emmy award-winning, animated **Star Trek**. In 1981, Filmation introduced **Blackstar**, an original sword and sorcery fantasy series which built up a following lasting well past its highly successful run on CBS.

Perhaps the highest praise from both critics and viewers were the accolades awarded **Fat Albert and the Cosby Kids**. In its unprecedented 12-year network run (followed in 1984 by 50 new episodes produced directly for syndication) *Fat Albert* was acclaimed by parents, educators and children alike for its entertaining blend of comedy and pro-social values. It has received countless honors, including several Emmy nominations and the prestigious Peabody Award.

In 1983, Filmation helped to create an entirely new marketplace for animated children's programming: first-run syndication. That year, the studio produced 65 episodes of **He-Man and the Masters of the Universe**. *He-Man* was an overnight sensation, garnering phenomenal ratings while drawing praise for its nonviolent stance and positive values. The "He-Man phenomenon" received extensive media coverage, including articles in the *New York Times* and *Time* magazine. The studio went on to produce 65 additional episodes of *He-Man* for broadcast through the 1986 season. And, to date, *He-Man* is being aired in 47 countries around the world.

ANIMATED SERIES FOR TELEVISION

AQUAMAN (WITH GUEST SUPER STARS: THE FLASH, GREEN LANTERN, HAWKMAN, TEEN TITANS, THE ATOM AND GREEN LANTERN)
ARCHIES, THE
ARCHIE'S FUNHOUSE
ARCHIES SPECIALS
ARCHIE'S TV FUNNIES

BATMAN AND ROBIN, THE ADVENTURES OF
BLACKSTARR
BRADY KIDS, THE
BRAVESTARR

FABULOUS FUNNIES, THE (WITH BROOM HILDA, ALLEY OOP, THE CAPTAIN AND THE KIDS, DICK TRACY AND EMMY LOU)
FANTASTIC VOYAGE
FAT ALBERT AND THE COSBY KIDS (WITH THE BROWN HORNET)
FAT ALBERT SPECIALS
FLASH GORDON, THE NEW ADVENTURES OF

GILLIGAN, THE NEW ADVENTURES OF
GILLIGAN'S PLANET
GHOST BUSTERS
GROOVIE GOOLIES, THE

HARDY BOYS, THE
HE-MAN AND THE MASTERS OF THE UNIVERSE

JOURNEY TO THE CENTER OF THE EARTH

KID SUPERPOWER HOUR WITH SHAZAM!

LASSIE AND THE RESCUE RANGERS
LONE RANGER, THE

MIGHTY MOUSE, THE NEW ADVENTURES OF (WITH HECKLE AND JECKLE)
MISSION: MAGIC!
MY FAVORITE MARTIANS

SABRINA, THE TEENAGE WITCH
SHE-RA, PRINCESS OF POWER
SPACE SENTINELS (ORIGINALLY CALLED THE YOUNG SENTINELS)
STAR TREK

SUPERMAN, THE NEW ADVENTURES OF (WITH SUPERBOY)

TARZAN, LORD OF THE JUNGLE
TARZAN AND THE SUPER7 (WITH WEB WOMAN, THE FREEDOM FORCE, MANTA AND MORAY, SUPERSTRETCH AND MICROWOMAN)
TARZAN, LONE RANGER, ZORRO ADVENTURE HOUR
TOM AND JERRY, THE NEW ADVENTURES OF (WITH DROOPY)

UNCLE CROC'S BLOCK (WITH FRAIDY CAT, M. U. S. H., WACKY AND PACKY AND WALDO KITTY)

WILL THE REAL JERRY LEWIS PLEASE SIT DOWN?
WALDO KITTY, THE NEW ADVENTURES OF

ZORRO, THE NEW ADVENTURES OF

HISTORY OF SHOWS

1966-1967
THE NEW ADVENTURES OF SUPERMAN (WITH SUPERBOY)

1967-1968
AQUAMAN / SUPERMAN HOUR OF ADVENTURE (WITH GUEST SUPER STARS)
JOURNEY TO THE CENTER OF THE EARTH

1968-1969
THE ARCHIES
BATMAN / SUPERMAN HOUR
FANTASTIC VOYAGE

1969-1970
ARCHIE'S COMEDY HOUR, STARRING SABRINA, THE TEENAGE WITCH
THE HARDY BOYS
SABRINA, THE TEENAGE WITCH

1970-1971
ARCHIE'S FUN HOUSE
WILL THE REAL JERRY LEWIS PLEASE SIT DOWN?
SABRINA AND THE GROOVIE GOOLIES

1971-1972
ARCHIE'S TV FUNNIES

1972-1973
FAT ALBERT AND THE COSBY KIDS
THE BRADY KIDS

1973-1974
EVERYTHING'S ARCHIE
MY FAVORITE MARTIANS

MISSION MAGIC
LASSIE'S RESCUE RANGERS
STAR TREK

1974 -1975
U.S. OF ARCHIE
SHAZAM! (LIVE ACTION)
THE NEW ADVENTURES OF GILLIGAN

1975-1976
SHAZAM-ISIS HOUR
GHOST BUSTERS (LIVE ACTION)
UNCLE CROC'S BLOCK (WITH FRAIDY CAT, M. U. S. H., WACKY AND PACKY AND WALDO KITTY)
THE ADVENTURES OF WALDO KITTY (ORIGINALLY CALLED THE SECRET LIVES OF WALDO KITTY)

1976-1977
TARZAN, LORD OF THE JUNGLE
ARK II (LIVE ACTION)
JOURNEY BACK TO OZ (SEEN DECEMBER 1976)
THE NEW ADVENTURES OF BATMAN

1977 - 1978
SPACE SENTINELS (ORIGINALLY CALLED THE YOUNG SENTINELS)
SPACE ACADEMY (LIVE ACTION)
THE BATMAN-TARZAN ADVENTURE HOUR
THE BANG SHANG LALAPALOOZA SHOW (STARRING ARCHIE)
THE SUPERWITCH SHOW (STARRING SABRINA)
FAT ALBERT HALLOWEEN SPECIAL
FAT ALBERT CHRISTMAS SPECIAL "SILENT KNIGHTS"

1978-1979
THE FABULOUS FUNNIES (WITH BROOM HILDA, ALLEY OOP, THE CAPTAIN AND THE KIDS, DICK TRACY, EMMY LOU)
TARZAN AND THE SUPER 7
JASON OF STAR COMMAND (LIVE ACTION)
SPACE ACADEMY (LIVE ACTION)

1979-1980
THE NEW ADVENTURES OF FLASH GORDON
FAT ALBERT AND THE COSBY KIDS (WITH THE BROWN HORNET)
THE NEW ADVENTURES OF MIGHTY MOUSE
FAT ALBERT EASTER SPECIAL
JASON, OF STAR COMMAND (LIVE ACTION)
A SNOW WHITE CHRISTMAS SPECIAL

1980-L981
THE NEW ADVENTURES OF TOM AND JERRY (WITH DROOPY)
SPORT BILLY (MADE FOR OVERSEAS)
FAT ALBERT "FOLLOW THE LEADER" (NUTRITIONAL SPOT TO BE SHOWN IN SCHOOLS)
FAT ALBERT DEPARTMENT OF ENERGY SPOT(SUBJECT: CONSERVATION)

1981-1982
TARZAN, LONE RANGER, ZORRO ADVENTURE HOUR
BLACKSTAR
THE KID SUPER POWER HOUR (WITH: HERO HIGH, SHAZAM! AND LIVE ACTION WRAP-A-ROUNDS)

1982-1983
GILLIGAN'S PLANET

1983-1985
HE-MAN AND THE MASTERS OF THE UNIVERSE

1985 - 1986
SHE-RA, THE PRINCESS OF POWER

1986 - 1987
GHOST BUSTERS (ANIMATED)

1987 - 1988
BRAVESTARR
BRAVESTARR THE LEGEND (ANIMATED MOVIE)

ANIMATED FEATURES

DAFFY DUCK AND PORKY PIG MEET THE GROOVIE GOOLIES- (1972) FEATURING DAFFY DUCK, PORKY PIG, DR. JEKYLL-MR. HYDE, NAPOLEON BONE-APART, WOLFIE, "FRANKIE" AND DRACFK.

JOURNEY BACK TO OZ - (1974) FEATURING DOROTHY, SCARECROW, COWARDLY LION, THE TIN MAN, WOODENHEAD PINTO STALLION III, THE SIGNPOST, PUMPKINHEAD.

OLIVER TWIST - (1981) FEATURING OLIVER TWIST, FAGIN.

TREASURE ISLAND - (1980)

MIGHTY MOUSE IN THE GREAT SPACE CHASE - (1982) FEATURING MIGHTY MOUSE, PEARL PUREHEART AND OIL CAN HARRY.

A CHRISTMAS SPECIAL- (1985) FEATURING HE-MAN, SHE-RA, SKELETOR, SORCERESS AND HORDAK, KOWL.

THE SECRET OF THE SWORD - (1985) FEATURING PRINCE ADAM (HE-MAN) AND PRINCESS ADORA (SHE-RA).

PINOCCHIO AND THE EMPEROR OF THE NIGHT- (1987) FEATURING PINOCCHIO, EMPEROR OF THE NIGHT, GEPPETTO, FAIRY GODMOTHER AND TWINKLE.

BRAVESTARR: THE LEGEND- (1988) FEATURING MARSHAL BRAVESTARR, DEPUTY FUZZ, HANDLEBAR, JUDGE B.J., OUTLAW SCUZZ, SHAMAN AND STAMPEDE.

HAPPILY EVER AFTER- (1990) FEATURING SNOW WHITE.

Animation by
FILMATION

AQUAMAN

Broadcast History:
THE SUPERMAN / AQUAMAN HOUR OF ADVENTURE
Network Premiere: CBS, September, 1967 Saturday Mornings

THE AQUAMAN SHOW
Network Premiere: CBS, September, 1968 Sunday Morning

Syndicated History:
SUPERMAN / BATMAN / AQUAMAN
Fall 1974

Executive Producer: Allen Ducovny
Producers: Louis Scheimer, Norman Prescott
Director: Hal Sutherland
Story Editor: Mort Weisinger
Art Director: Don Christensen

Principal Characters and Voices:
AQUAMAN...Marvin Miller
AQUALAD..Jerry Dexter
MERA..Diana Maddox
STORM (Aquaman's seahorse) / IMP (Aqualad's sea pony) / TUSKY (Aqualad's pet walrus) / NARRATOR / VILLAINS....
....Ted Knight
THE FLASH..Cliff Owens
KID FLASH ....Tommy Cook
WONDER GIRL..Julie Bennett
HAWKMAN..Gilbert Mack
THE ATOM / SPEEDY ....Pat Harrington, Jr.
GREEN LANTERN ....Gerald Mohr
KYRO / GUARDIAN OF THE UNIVERSE.....,,....Paul Frees

Aquaman, known to his comic book fans as "The King of the Seven Seas," was the second DC Comics' superhero from the print media adapted for Saturday morning. The aquatic star had been preceded for one season by Superman and was first teamed in Filmation's *The Superman/Aquaman Hour of Adventure* for the CBS network.

The overwhelming success of Filmation's premiere alliance with National Periodical Publications (later called DC Comics) on their *New Adventures of Superman* series led to the two companies seeking to further that alliance. CBS gave them an additional half hour for the following season, and National opened its impressive library of superhero characters as potential stars for the new half-hour. Among the heroes developed were: *Blackhawk, Plastic Man, Wonder Woman, the Challengers of the Unknown, The Metal Men, B'wana Beast,* and *Metamorpho, the Element Man.*

It was decided that, since Superman and Superboy's adventures took place on the surface of and above the surface of the Earth, a series starring Superman's aquatic counterpart, Aquaman, would, with his adventures set below Earth's oceans, provide a visual contrast to the other half hour. Aquaman often rode into action on his seahorse, Storm, and Aqualad on

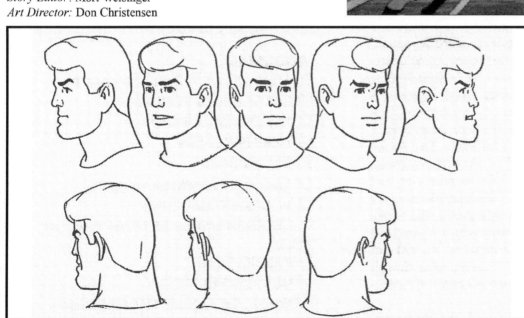

his sea pony, Imp, accompanied by Tusky, the lad's pet walrus. Such villains as Black Manta (an underwater sea pirate), the Brain, the Mirror Men, the Merman, the Torpedo, and others challenged Aquaman.

Despite some liberties taken with the characters' visual designs and the addition of seahorse pets Storm and Imp and comedy relief pet Tusky to the cast, the series stayed fairly close to its comics of Aquaman's animated exploits. The writer of the Aquaman comics, Bob Haney, scripted many of these.

The format of the series, now called *The Superman/Aquaman Hour of Adventure* began with a six minute Aquaman adventure and was followed by a Superman adventure, then a Superboy segment. Interspersed with these three segments were 30-second "secret code messages" which the young home viewer would decipher using the special "code-alphabet" to learn who would star in the series' fourth segment. A revolving portion featured one of six other concepts that had also been developed for series that season. Those super-guest stars were: The Flash, The Atom, Green Lantern, Hawkman, The Teen Titans (team members were Aqualad, Kid Flash, Wonder Girl, and Speedy, who was used because Filmation did not have the rights to Robin who was a member at the time), and the Justice League of America, which teamed the other super-guest stars with Superman but did not include The Teen Titans and Aquaman, even though Aquaman was featured in the *Justice League of America* segment's opening titles.

The Atom was a DC Comics character that appeared as a segment of the *Superman/Aquaman Hour*. Created by DC Comics in the early 60s, the Atom's name came from a short, but strong golden age DC hero who had no superpowers. The newer version of the Atom had the power to shrink down to microscopic sizes. Adding to the effectiveness of this power, he could also change his weight from his normal weight to next to nothing and back again. When his weight matched his small size, he could practically fly by using even minimal wind power. When he wanted to attack a bad guy, he could use his normal weight to pack a mean punch.

Like all of the other DC hero segments, the stories were fairly generic in nature, so none of them really stood out.

Another of the rotating segments on the *Superman/Aquaman Hour of Adventure* was the *Teen Titans* based on the DC Comics of the same name. The Titans were a junior version of the *Justice League of the America* which included Robin, Batman's ward/side-kick; Aqualad, Aquaman's sidekick; Speedy, the Green Arrow's side-kick; Wonder Girl, Wonder Woman's younger sister; and Kid Flash, the Flash's nephew and occasional partner. All of the Titans were present in the cartoon version,

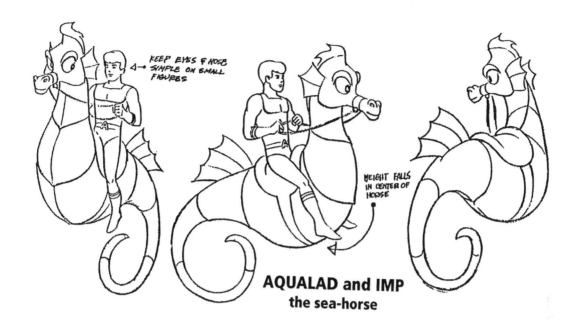

AQUALAD and IMP
the sea-horse

TUSKY
the pet walrus

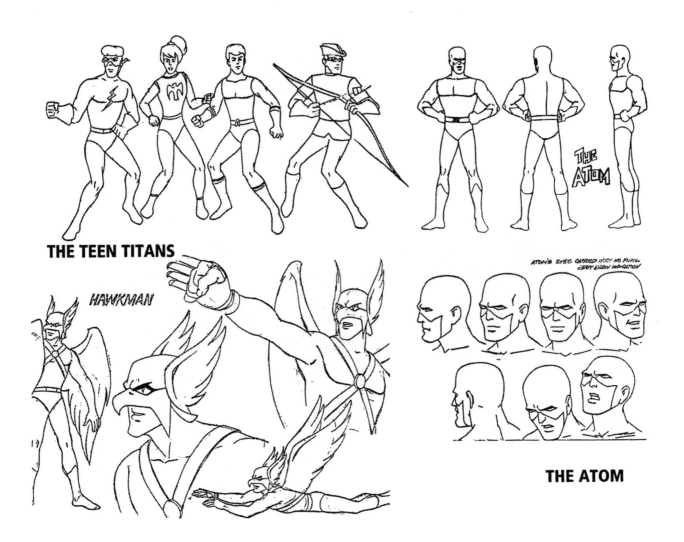

THE TEEN TITANS

HAWKMAN

THE ATOM

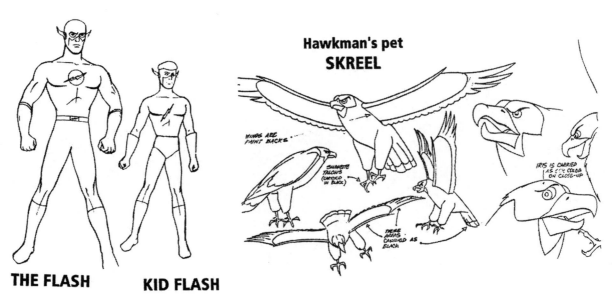

THE FLASH **KID FLASH**

Hawkman's pet **SKREEL**

©1967 DC Comics

with the exception of Robin, the boy wonder. Filmation didn't have the rights for the character at that time (the following year, Filmation got the rights for Robin and he became part of their *Batman* series).

In the comics, the Teen Titans, Robin, kid Flash and Aqualad, originally got together to stop the Justice League of America, who had been turned evil by aliens. Since they worked well togther, they met up together on a regular basis. The basic premise of the Teen Titans was kept intact in the animated version. Their headquarters were based in a hollowed out section of a mountain. When a situation arose that needed their attention, they would contact each other and set about solving the problem/ capturing the crooks. Once they completed their adventures, they departed until they were needed again.

Like the other rotating segments, the *Teen Titans* were fairly routine in both story and animation. Yet none of the part time Titans (Hawk and Dove, Lillith, Beast Boy, etc...) or any of the comic book villans made an appearance on the show.

Although Wonder Girl and Speedy were included in this series, their adult counterparts, Wonder Woman and the Green Arrow, were not part of the animated *Justice Leaque of America* or one of the other animated segments on the *Superman/ Aquaman Hour*. Althought, a few years later, Wonder Woman made her first animated appearance in an episode of the *Brady Kids*, before joining Batman, Superman, Aquaman, and Robin in Hanna Barbera's version of the *Justice League of America*, *Super Friends*. Green Arrow never appeared in any Filmation cartoon and to this date, his only animated appearance was as a guest star on the first season of the *Super Friends*.

Beginning in September, 1968, Aquaman was repeated in own half-hour series containing two of his adventures and one with the guest superheroes.

(Author's Note: One guest star hero, Metamorpho, supposedly went as far as a fully commissioned, animated half-hour. Reports conflict between National and Filmation as to whether the episode, which retold the Element Man's origin, was actually produced..)

AQUAMAN
☐ MENACE OF THE BLACK MANTA
☐ RAMPAGING REPTILE MEN
☐ RETURN OF NEPTRO
☐ FIERY INVADERS
☐ SEA RAIDERS
☐ WAR OF THE WATER WORLDS
☐ VOLCANIC MONSTER
☐ CRIMSON MONSTER FROM THE PINK POOL
☐ ICE DRAGON
☐ DEADLY DRILLERS

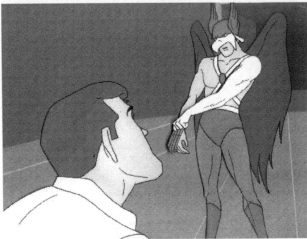

- [ ] IN CAPTAIN 'CUDA'S CLUTCHES
- [ ] THE MIRROR-MEN FROM PLANET IMAGO
- [ ] THE SEA SORCERER
- [ ] THE SEA SNARES OF CAPTAIN SLY

JUSTICE LEAGUE OF AMERICA
- [ ] BETWEEN TWO ARMIES
- [ ] TARGET EARTH
- [ ] BAD DAY ON BLACK MOUNTAIN

THE ATOM
- [ ] INVASION OF THE BEETLE PEOPLE
- [ ] THE PLANT MACHINE
- [ ] HOUSE OF DOOM

THE TEEN TITANS
- [ ] THE MONSTER MACHINE
- [ ] THE GREAT SPACE-BEAST ROUNDUP
- [ ] OPERATION RESCUE

THE FLASH
- [ ] THE CHEMO CREATURE
- [ ] TAKE A GIANT STEP
- [ ] TO CATCH A BLUE BOLT

HAWKMAN
- [ ] PERIL FROM PLUTO
- [ ] A VISIT TO VENUS
- [ ] THE TWENTY-THIRD DIMENSION

GREEN LANTERN
- [ ] EVIL IS AS EVIL DOES
- [ ] THE VANISHING WORLD
- [ ] SIRENA - EMPRESS OF EVIL

- [ ] VASSA - QUEEN OF THE MERMAN
- [ ] MICROSCOPIC MONSTER
- [ ] ONSLAUGHT OF THE OCTOMEN
- [ ] TREACHEROUS IS THE TORPEDOMAN
- [ ] SATANIC SATURIANS
- [ ] THE BRAIN, THE BRAVE, AND THE BOLD
- [ ] WHERE LURKS THE FISHERMAN
- [ ] MEPHISTO'S MARINE MARAUDERS
- [ ] THE TRIO OF TERROR
- [ ] THE TORP, THE MAGNETO, AND THE CLAW
- [ ] GOLIATHS OF THE DEEP-SEA GORGE
- [ ] SINISTER SEA SCAMP
- [ ] SEA DEVIL
- [ ] THE SEA SCAVENGERS
- [ ] THE UNDERSEA TROJAN HORSE
- [ ] THE VICIOUS VILLAINY OF VASSA
- [ ] PROGRAMMED FOR DESTRUCTION
- [ ] THE SILVER SPHERE
- [ ] TO CATCH A FISHERMAN
- [ ] THE WAR OF THE QUATIX AND THE BIMPH-ADS
- [ ] THE STICKMAN OF STYGIA
- [ ] THREE WISHES TO TROUBLE

THE ARCHIES

Broadcast History:
THE ARCHIE SHOW
Network Premiere: CBS, September, 1968 Saturday Mornings

Producers: Norm Prescott, Lou Schiemer
Director: Hal Sutherland
Art Director: Don Christensen
Writer: Bob Ogle

THE ARCHIE COMEDY HOUR
Network Premiere: CBS, September, 1969 Saturday Mornings
Producers: Norm Prescott, Lou Schiemer
Director: Hal Sutherland
Art Director: Don Christensen
Writers: Bob Ogle, Jim Mulligan, Jim Ryan, Bill Danch, Jack Mendelson, Chuck Menville, Len Jansen

ARCHIE'S FUNHOUSE
Network Premiere: CBS, September, 1970, Saturday Mornings
Producers: Norm Prescott, Lou Schiemer
Director: Hal Sutherland
Art Director: Don Christensen
Writers: Jim Ryan, Bill Danch

ARCHIE'S TV FUNNIES
Network Premiere: CBS, September, 1971 Saturday Mornings
Producers: Norm Prescott, Lou Schiemer
Director: Hal Sutherland
Art Director: Don Christensen
Writers: Jim Ryan, Bill Danch, Ken Sobol

EVERYTHING'S ARCHIE
Network Premiere: CBS, September, 1973 Saturday Mornings

THE U. S. OF ARCHIE
Network Premiere: CBS, September, 1974 Saturday Mornings
Executive Producers: Norm Prescott, Lou Schiemer
Creative Producer: Don Christensen
Directors: Lou Zukor, Don Towsley, Bill Reed
Writers: Chuck Menville, Len Jenson, Bill Danch, Jim Ryan, Marc Richards

THE NEW ARCHIE / SABRINA HOUR
Network Premiere: NBC, September, 1977 Saturday Mornings
Executive Producers: Norm Prescott, Lou Schiemer
Producer: Don Christensen

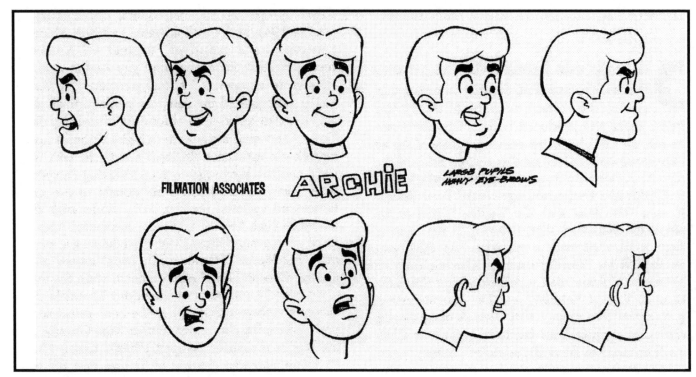

Director: Marsh Lamore, Don Towsley, Rudy Larriva
Associate Producers / Story Editors: Jim Ryan, Bill Danch
THE BANG-SHANG LALAPALOOZA SHOW
Network Premiere: NBC, November, 1977 Saturday Mornings
Executive Producers: Lou Scheimer, Norm Prescott
Producer: Hal Sutherland
Creative Director: Don Christensen
Directors: Don Towsley, Lou Zukor, Rudy Larriva, Bill Reed

Principal Characters: and Voices:
ARCHIE ANDREWS / HOT DOG / MR. WEATHERBEE / COACH CLEATS / CHUCK CLAYTON / CAPTAIN HANS / GAYLORD / SAM KETCHUM / KAYO / ALF / COUSIN / AMBROSE / CHIEF / MR. ANDREWS / MR. LODGE / SALEM / PAT PATTON / CHILI DOG / B.O. PLENTY..Dallas McKennon
JUGHEAD JONES /BIG MOOSE / POPS / FRANKIE / WOLFIE / MUMMY / GHOULAHAND / INSPECTOR / FRITZ JUNIOR / SLUGGO / SANDY / DILTON DOILY / MOON MULLINS / FOO CAT / HOT DOG JR..……......……Howard Morris
BETTY COOPER / VERONICA LODGE / BIG ETHEL / MISS GRUNDY / SABRINA / AUNT HILDA / AUNT ZELDA / HAGATHA / BELLA LA GHOSTLY / BROOM-HILDA / NANCY / MAMA / MISS DELLA / FRITZI RITZ, GRAVEL GERTIE.…..............………….………………Jane Webb
REGGIE MANTLE / HEXSTER / DICK TRACY ALVIN / SMOKEY / STOVER / IRWIN / DAD ....John Erwin
COUNT DRAC / BATSO / GOOLIHAND...............Larry Storch
CARLOS..Jose Flores
OPHELIA .... Treva Frazce
HARVEY .... Don Messick

One of the most successful and imitated series that ever appeared on Saturday morning television, the various versions of the Archie Comics' characters produced under Filmation's auspices ran on CBS for eight seasons, followed by an additional run on NBC for another season. Bringing the Archie characters to television was the brainchild of CBS Children's Programming wizard Fred Silverman…aka "The Man with the Golden Gut" (via his admirers and detractors alike, referring to his uncanny instincts as to what made a television hit). Silverman strove to shift his Saturday morning schedule from its emphasis on "violence" and superheroes after the assassination of Robert Kennedy and Dr. Martin Luther King Jr. earlier that year (1968). This ideology caused newly found organizations (such as Action for Children's Television) to decry the so-called "violent" trend in kid's cartoons. Ironically, the last superhero series that CBS bought that season was the most "vio-

lent" of them all: Filmation's *Batman/Superman Hour*.

Silverman, going by his instincts as well as the demographic testing he instigated, surmised that his target audience (2-11 year olds) fantasized being the age of their older brothers and sisters: high school age. With this in mind, he commissioned Filmation to create an animated series based on the popular Archie comic books. Also contributing to this action was Filmation's track record of success with previous DC Comics' properties. The long-running comic book, created in 1941 by John Goldwater and Bob Montana, centered on a group of "typical all-American teenagers:" straight arrow good guy Archie Andrews (known to exasperated school personnel as "Archi-bald"), who juggled the dauntless perils of final exams and his two girlfriends—blonde and bouncy Betty Cooper and spoiled southern rich-girl Veronica Lodge; rat-fink par excellence Reginald Mantle III (aka "Reggie"); and the hamburger-loving/girl-hating Forsythe P. Jones (aka "Jughead"). All were brought to the screen intact and updated for the '60's, along with their Riverdale High friends: Jughead's unrequited love, Big Ethyl; class genius Dilton Doiy; class dunce and strongman "Big Moose" Manson; and "Pops," owner of the nearby "Choc'lit Shop." Also on board were the sometimes friendly, sometimes contentious Riverdale High faculty members: the stuffy, by-the-book principal Mr. Weatherbee; frazzled senior teacher Miss Grundy; and the biggest rah-rah on campus, athletic Coach Cleats. Filmation added an element of its own into the mix: Jughead's dog Hot Dog who, in a rarity for animated dogs, never spoke (the audience heard his thoughts as he wryly commented on the events taking place around him). Another unusual thing about the canine was that he (Hot Dog) really thought he was "human."

It was another Filmation addition, however, that elevated *The Archie Show*, the title of Filmation's first Archie incarnation, from being just another Saturday morning kid's cartoon to that of a true nationwide pop phenomenon.

It was decided that, to contemporize the Archie gang for the "modern-day kids" audience and teens, CBS would bring in famed music producer Don Kirshner (who, among his other accomplishments, put together the "pre-fab four"—The Monkees…his answer to The Beatles) to bring the same type of "magic" to this new enterprise. Kirshner's previous musical experience with The Monkees ended on a sour note as his pre-Kirshner musicians grew confident and talented enough over time to eventually fire Kirshner and take over the production of their own music. Partly to assuage his own ego, and partly to get revenge on these "living musicians," Kirshner strove to prove that he could make the ultimate "pre-fab four" by using rock singers who were not even real, a la Ross Bagdasarian's early 1960's combo, David Seville and the Chipmunks. So, using a similar format in *The Archie Show*, Kirshner hired musician Ron Dante to provide (by means of re-recording) all the harmonies for a segment that would appear in the middle of each Archie Show half hour. This featured the Archie cast as a pop

band called "The Archies." With Archie on lead guitar, Reggie on bass, Betty on tambourine, Veronica on the organ, Jughead on the drums, and Hot Dog as "conductor," the band sang a new ditty each episode, accompanied by the "Dance of the Week" in which a fun new dance was introduced each week for the kids to do at home. Each Archie cast member had a special dance...even dances such as "The Grundy" and "The Weatherbee" showed up. Other dances included the "Hamburger Hop," the "Stickshift," and the now politically incorrect "The Indian." With two Archie stories bracketing the songs, The Archie Show hit the airwaves in September of 1968. Within a few weeks, The Archie Show scored some of the highest shares ever reached on Saturday mornings or television in general: they hit a phenomenal 55 share at one point (in comparison to today's television where a 25 share is seen as "hit" status...and very seldom reached. Even more phenomenal, however, was the success of The Archies singing group as their album, released under Kirshner's label, reached "platinum" status along with several Archie singles. Hit songs included "Bang-Shang-a-Lang" and "Jingle Jangle." One single, "Sugar Sugar," not only hit platinum but also was the top selling single of 1969 on the Billboard charts. It sold over five million copies and became a music staple (as well as serving as Kirshner's "vindication" over his former Monkee associates).

Another CBS/Filmation creative addition made its "magic" known—quite literally—the following season (1969 1970) when CBS, responding to The Archie Show's overwhelming success, wanted to expand the concept to an hour. After unsuccessfully attempting to secure the rights for an animated version of the popular *Bewitched* series (partly, one assumes, because the live-action witch comedy aired on rival ABC), CBS, Silverman, and Filmation created their own version of the concept. Sabrina, the teen-age witch, joined the Archie gang in its escapades during two segments of the expanded format... now called *The Archie Comedy Hour*. CBS was so excited about the character that, for the first time, they commissioned an all-new half-hour prime time animated special to showcase the character. In the special, *Archie and His New Pals* (laid out by future feature producer Don Bluth, whose dynamic Disney-influenced layout style combined with the usually staid Filmation approach to create some truly interesting visuals), the politics of a high school election served as the catalyst for the arrival of Sabrina to the town of Riverdale. The show was re-broadcast a year later as Archie's *Sugar Sugar/Jingle Jangle Show* and re-edited to add The Archies' two new top ten tunes. Seizing upon an equal opportunity to borrow a hit concept from his other network rival, NBC, Silverman and Filmation created two fast-paced segments for *The Archie Comedy Hour*... the "Funhouse" and the "Side Show". They each featured the Archie gang in a rapid-fire mix of sight-gags, comic skits, and lame puns which all bore remarkable similarities to NBC's primetime hit *Rowan and Martin's Laugh-In* (to ensure the same pacing and style, they even hired

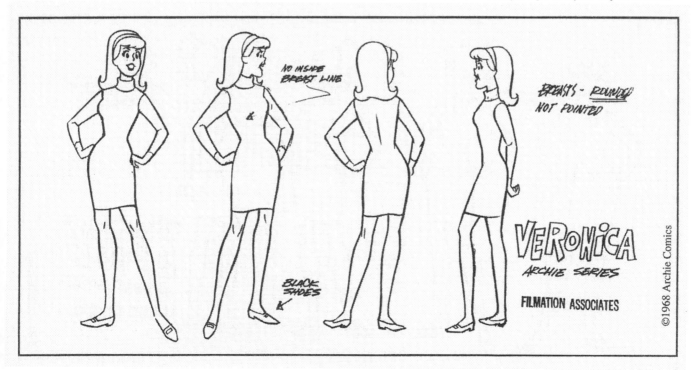

two *Laugh-In* writers, Jack Mendelsohn and Jim Mulligan, to script the segments). So popular were the new additions to the Archie format that the following season (1970-'71) *Sabrina* and *Archie's Funhouse* were both spun-off into hour-length series of their own which bracketed the number one CBS Saturday morning schedule that season...not to mention heavily influencing the other series on CBS' line-up—all produced by rival production house Hanna-Barbera. One was even used as the basis for another Archie comic book. Having their production facilities overbooked with beyond two-and-a-half hours of new weekly programming that year *(Sabrina, Archie's Funhouse,* and ABC's *Will the Real Jerry Lewis, Please Sit Down?)*, fellow Archie Group comic *Josie and the Pussycats* had to be given to Hanna-Barbera to produce.

The Archie's musical influence was strongly felt, not just in *Josie and the Pussycats,* which focused on the comedic around-the-world exploits of a teenage pop band, but also in Hanna-Barbera's *Harlem Globetrotters*, which used Archie music producer Don Kirshner to produce the pop tunes played during the animated Trotter's games. Such pop tunes even showed up during the chase sequences of Hanna-Barbera's comedy mystery series, *Scooby Doo, Where Are You!*

The following season (1971-'72) saw an entirely different direction taken by CBS and Filmation in regards to the Archie gang. *The Archie's Funhouse* half-hours were spun off into the CBS Sunday rerun slot (aside from its five-hour Saturday line up, the network used the 7-8 AM slot on Sunday mornings to rerun some of its previous Saturday morning occupants), and the remaining Saturday half-hour became the repository for a large variety of recent Filmation rights acquisitions. *Archie's TV Funnies* took the Archie gang from the environs of Riverdale High, the Fun House, and the Choc'lit Shop, and placed the kids in charge of running the town's TV station, which, in exterior shots, looked uncannily like Filmation's studio building at the time on Sherman Way and Langley Avenue in Reseda, California. Incidentally, this was where Filmation got the name for its music-publishing wing—Shermley Music Corp. The Archie kids ran programming for the station, which mainly consisted of their various story-chasing antics in the last segment and the adventures of varied comic strip characters in the first two. First segments featured Broom Hilda and the Captain and the Kids while the second segments featured *Dick Tracy, Emmy Lou, Nancy and Sluggo, Moon Mullins, The Dropouts,* and *Smokey Stover*. This series ran for two seasons with a reformatted rerun package combining edited clips from all of the previous Archie series running on Saturdays as *Everything's Archie*. In 1974, Filmation (which, because of the critical acclaim being bestowed on its *Fat Albert* series pushed the demand for more shows with pro-social/educational content) was asked by one of the CBS programming heads if it could develop, with thoughts

leaning toward the upcoming American Bicentennial Celebration of 1976, a series that would teach kids about American history in an entertaining fashion. From this request came 1974's *U.S. of Archie*, in which the Archie gang, (including its first integrated member, black friend Chuck Clayton,) portrayed its "ancestors" (all named by the same names the current kids used), meeting and interacting with various movers and shakers in American history. Such icons included Paul Revere, Benjamin Franklin, Lewis and Clark, George Washington Carver, and Harriet Tubman. Historically themed songs were supplied by a new Archies "group" (Kirshner and Dante having moved to supply songs and vocals for Hanna-Barbera's *Amazing Chan and Chan Clan*) and producer Jackie Mills, who served as *The Brady Kids* music producer. This series, however, was not as successful as *The Archies'* previous efforts. It was not only cancelled in 1976, ending *The Archies* eight-year run on CBS, but was ironically dumped six months before the Bicentennial Celebration the show had been created for in the first place.

That September (1976), the entire *Archie* package (including the *Sabrina* shows) was put into the syndication marketplace and featured what could almost be considered one of the first mainstream examples of "rap" music as most of *The Archie Comedy Hour* song segments were re-looped with Dallas McKennon's Archie character talking through the bouncy visuals. The show did so well in syndication that unofficial "godfather" Fred Silverman, who was now head of NBC network programming, ordered a brand-new hour of Archie gang antics under the cognomen: *The New Archie/Sabrina Hour* (1977). This show pretty much went back to the tried and true story format with the first twelve minutes featuring a new *Sabrina* segment (with a major story change however: in this segment Sabrina's magic was used more openly, and she spent most of her time using magic to make everybody forget she had used it in the first place). The second segments were half-hour *New Archie* stories with the third segment titled *Surprise Packages*. They were basically no surprise in that they featured the same casts in the same old story situations. Two new characters joined the Archie cast: replacing the black character Chuck, in a spirit of racial equanimity, was the Hispanic teen Carlos, who was an artistic free spirit; and, to serve as "homage" to the then-new *Star Wars* movie's R2-D2 and C-3PO robots was Dilton's "Q," a little robot acquired from NASA (though this was later revised to have been built by the

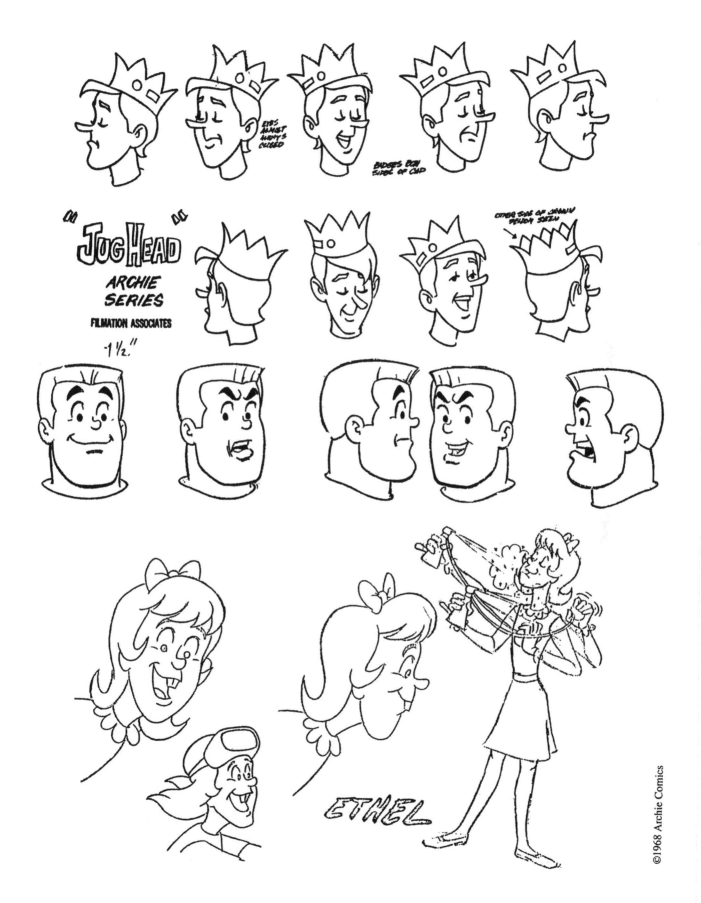

boy inventor). Unfortunately, the old format, even with two new Archie songs each week (still produced by the Jackie Mill's team and more reliant on redressed Filmation stock animation: the characters didn't even "lip-sync" this time around), scored lackluster ratings. This necessitated a separation after eight weeks into two half-hours. *The new Sabrina* and *Surprise Package* segments were all reformatted into *Super Witch* while *The New Archie* half-hours became (ready?) *The Bang-Shang Lalapalooza Show* starring Archie and his Gang. They actually fit all of that onto one title card! But the retitling, along with Filmation's retitling its *Young Sentinels* as *Space Sentinels*, didn't help as all three shows were cancelled that season (and ironically, Hanna-Barbera became NBC's principal supplier the following season).

Filmation almost became involved with still another Archie concept when it developed a possible *Super Archies* series based on the Pureheart the Powerful, Captain Hero, and other characters the Archie kids sometimes became. This was later altered, partly for ownership reasons (Filmation got to own it, plus being paired with another previously established concept), into *The Kid Super Power Hour with Shazam!* series that aired on NBC in 1981.

During their eight seasons on network television, *The Archies* influenced the television landscape in ways that few series did before or have since.

THE ARCHIE SHOW (1968)
- [ ] THE ADDED DISTRACTION
- [ ] WHO IS AFRAID OF REGGIE WOLF
- [ ] A HARD DAY'S KNIGHT
- [ ] CHIMP OFF THE OLD BLOCK
- [ ] BEAUTY IS ONLY FUR DEEP
- [ ] THE DISAPPEARING ACT
- [ ] THE PRIZE WINNER
- [ ] THE CIRCUS
- [ ] HOT ROD DRAG
- [ ] JUGHEAD'S DOUBLE
- [ ] THE GREAT MARATHON
- [ ] FIELD TRIP
- [ ] SNOW BUSINESS
- [ ] ANCHOR'S AWAY
- [ ] WAY-OUT LIKE WEST
- [ ] FLYING SAUCERS

- ☐ THE COMPUTER
- ☐ JUGHEAD SIMPSON JONES
- ☐ KIDS DAY
- ☐ PAR ONE PFC HOT DOG
- ☐ GROOVY GHOST
- ☐ ROCKET ROCK
- ☐ THE OLD SEA DOG
- ☐ JUGHEAD'S GIRL
- ☐ DILTON'S FOLLY
- ☐ PRIVATE EYE JUGHEAD
- ☐ STRIKE THREE
- ☐ REGGIE'S COUSIN
- ☐ CAT NEXT DOOR
- ☐ THE JONES FARM
- ☐ VERONICA'S VEIL

ARCHIE'S TV FUNNIES (1971) episodes
- ☐ ESCAPED HIPPO
- ☐ FLYING SAUCER
- ☐ BANK ROBBERY
- ☐ WACKY RACES-ARCHIE STYLE
- ☐ AIR CIRCUS
- ☐ THE GHOST OF SWEDLOW SWAMP
- ☐ RIVERDALE TALENT TOURNAMENT
- ☐ RODNEY RINKYDINK
- ☐ MOUNT RIVERDALE WOODS
- ☐ THE REGGIE GAME
- ☐ MOM'S CHICKEN SICKLE STAND
- ☐ OUR TOWN, RIVERDALE
- ☐ OUTSIDE INTERFERENCE

U.S. OF ARCHIE (1974)
- ☐ UNDERGROUND RAILROAD
- ☐ GOLD
- ☐ THE DAY OF THE LADIES
- ☐ THE STAR SPANGLED BANNER
- ☐ THE WRIGHT BROTHERS
- ☐ THE ROUGHRIDERS
- ☐ THE GOLDEN SPIKE
- ☐ FLAME OF FREEDOM
- ☐ THERE SHE BLOWS
- ☐ BEN FRANKLIN AND THE POST OFFICE
- ☐ THE RIVER
- ☐ MR. WATSON, COME HERE
- ☐ THE CRIME OF IGNORANCE
- ☐ THE GREAT DIVIDE
- ☐ FULTON'S FOLLY
- ☐ WIZARD OF MENLO PARK

THE NEW ARCHIES (1977)
- ☐ CHIEF ARCHIE
- ☐ ME AND MY SHADOW
- ☐ THERE'S NO PLACE LIKE OUTER SPACE
- ☐ A MOVING EXPERIENCE
- ☐ ROBERT BLUEFORD
- ☐ TOPS IN COPS
- ☐ TRACK AND FIELD
- ☐ WHERE THERE'S SMOKE
- ☐ ARCHIE'S MILLIONS
- ☐ CAREER DAY
- ☐ THE QUIXOTE CAPER
- ☐ PIRATE KEY
- ☐ ON THE "Q" TEE

BATMAN AND ROBIN

Broadcast History:
THE BATMAN / SUPERMAN HOUR
Network Premiere: CBS, September, 1968 Saturday Mornings

THE ADVENTURES OF BATMAN AND ROBIN
Network Premiere: CBS, September, 1969 Saturday Mornings
THE NEW ADVENTURES OF BATMAN
Network Premiere: CBS, February, 1977 Saturday Mornings
THE BATMAN / TARZAN ADVENTURE HOUR
Network Premiere: CBS, September, 1977 Saturday Mornings
TARZAN AND THE SUPER 7

BATMAN
©1968 DC Comics

Network Premiere: CBS, September, 1978 Saturday Mornings
BATMAN AND THE SUPER 7
Network Premiere: NBC, September, 1980 Saturday Mornings

Syndicated History:
SUPERMAN / AQUAMAN / BATMAN
Syndication Premiere: Fall, 1977

Executive Producers: Norman Prescott, Louis Scheimer, Allen Ducovny
Producers: Norman Prescott, Louis Scheimer (1968-1969), Don Christensen (1977)
Directors: Hal Sutherland (1968-1969), Don Towsley (1977)

Principal Characters and Voices:
BATMAN / BRUCE WAYNE ....
...............................(1968-69) Olan Soule, (1977) Adam West
ROBIN / DICK GRAYSON...
...............,,,,..............(1968-69) Casey Kasem, (1977) Burt Ward
BATGIRL / BARBARA GORDON / CAT-WOMAN................
................................(1968-69) Jane Webb, (1977) Melendy Britt
ALFRED PENNYWORTH / COMMISSIONER GORDON / JOKER / PENGUIN / RIDDLER / MR FREEZE / SIMON THE PIEMAN / NARRATOR ....(1968-69) Ted Knight
BATMITE ....Lou Scheimer
JOKER / PENGUIN / RIDDLER / MR. FREEZE / ELECTRO / CHAMELEON / ZARBOR / CLAY-FACE / MOONMAN / SWEETOOTH / PROFESSOR BUBBLES / COMMISSIONER GORDON .... (1977) Lennie Weinrib

Batman and Robin became the animated crime fighters in *The Adventures of Batman and Robin* (1968), tangling with infamous criminals who broke the law in Gotham City. Secretly known only to their loyal butler, Alfred, as the town's masked peacekeepers, clean-cut millionaire-philanthropist Bruce Wayne and Dick Grayson, his teenage ward, occupied their time in stately Wayne Manor until a Bat-signal from the police Commissioner Gordon would summon them to action. One two-part action story was seen in each episode along with a second six-minute tale. The pair were sometimes joined by Batgirl, Commissioner Gordon's daughter, Barbara. Creating problems for the Bat-trio with infernal, crime-like skullduggery were such Batfoes as the Riddler, Catwoman, Simon the Pieman, the frigid Mr. Freeze, that pudgy purveyor of perfidy, the Penguin, and the clown prince of crime, the Joker.

Following a seven-year network hiatus from being featured in his own series, Bat-Mite, a simian-like supermascot, replaced Alfred and provided prankish monkeyshines in *The New Adventures of Batman*. Seemingly unjailable, still at large, and causing chaos were the Penguin, the Joker, the Riddler, and Catwoman. The half-hour stories also featured the schemes of Clayface, the Chameleon, Electro, the sugar-happy crook, Sweet Tooth, and the Moon Man, an astronaut who became a criminal every full moon.

Since Hanna-Barbera was also producing *The Superfriends* for ABC with Batman and Robin as characters at the time, this marked one of the few times in animation history that two studios, Hanna-Barbera and Filmation, simultaneously produced stories with the same characters on two different networks.

Interestingly, while Hanna-Barbera's Dynamic Duo were portrayed by the late '60's Bat-voices of Olan Soule and Casey Kasem, Filmation recruited the 1960's live Bat-actors, Adam West and Burt Ward, to provide the voices to their animated counterparts for the '70's version.

ADVENTURES OF BATMAN AND ROBIN (1968)
☐ MY CRIME IS YOUR CRIME
☐ THE COOL, CRUEL MR. FREEZE
☐ HOW MANY HERRINGS IN A WHEEL BARROW
☐ THE NINE LIVES OF BATMAN
☐ BUBI, BUBI, WHO'S GOT THE RUBY
☐ BIG BIRTHDAY CAPER
☐ PARTNERS IN CRIME
☐ HIZZONER THE JOKER (JOKER FOR MAYOR)
☐ THE JIGSAW JEOPARDY
☐ IT TAKES TWO TO MAKE A TEAM
☐ THE CRIME COMPUTER
☐ A GAME OF CAT AND MOUSE
☐ OPERA BUFFA
☐ WILL THE REAL ROBIN PLEASE STAND UP?
☐ SIMON, THE PIEMAN
☐ CATWOMAN, BE MY VALENTINE
☐ A PERFIDIOUS PIEMAN IS SIMON
☐ THE FIENDISH, FRIGID FRAUD
☐ THE JIGSAW JEOPARDY
☐ BIRD OUT OF HAND
☐ THE JOKE'S ON ROBIN
☐ IN AGAIN, OUT AGAIN, PENGUIN
☐ LONG JOHN JOKER
☐ 1001 FACES OF THE RIDDLER
☐ TWO PENGUINS TOO MANY
☐ THE UNDERWORLD, UNDERGROUND CAPER
☐ MR. FREEZE'S FROZEN VIKINGS
☐ THE GREAT SCARECROW SCARE
☐ BEWARE OF LIVING DOLLS
☐ HE WHO SWIPES THE ICE GOES TO THE COOLER
☐ A MAD, MAD TEA PARTY
☐ PERILOUS PLAYTHINGS

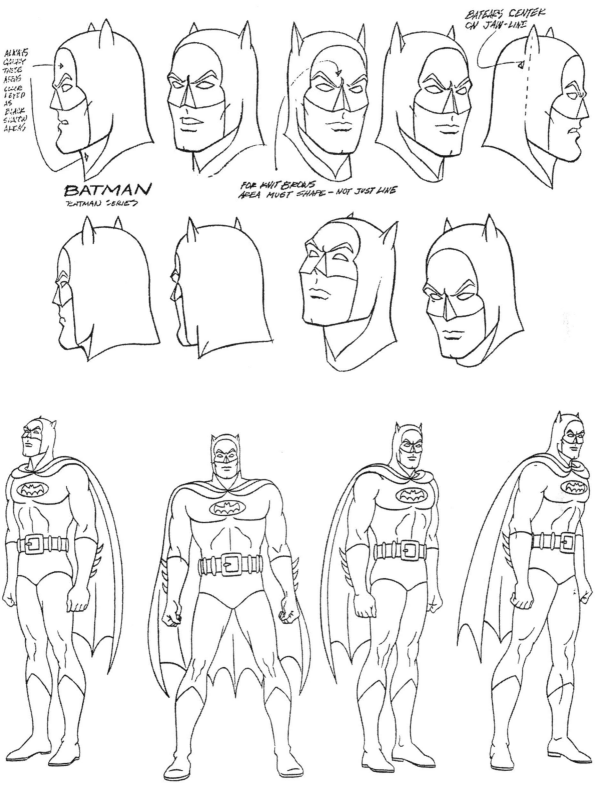

model sheet of
BATMAN

- ☐ THE COOL, CRUEL CHRISTMAS CAPER
- ☐ ENTER THE JUDGE
- ☐ WRATH OF THE RIDDLER

THE NEW ADVENTURES OF BATMAN (1977)
- ☐ THE PEST
- ☐ THE MOONMAN
- ☐ TROUBLE IDENTITY
- ☐ A SWEET JOKE ON GOTHAM CITY
- ☐ THE BERMUDA RECTANGLE
- ☐ CURSES! OILED AGAIN!
- ☐ BITE-SIZED
- ☐ READING, WRITING & WRONGING
- ☐ THE CHAMELEON
- ☐ HE WHO LAUGHS LAST
- ☐ THE DEEP FREEZE
- ☐ DEAD RINGERS
- ☐ BIRDS OF A FEATHER FOOL AROUND TOGETHER
- ☐ HAVE AN EVIL DAY (PART I - II)
- ☐ THIS LOOKS LIKE A JOB FOR BAT-MITE

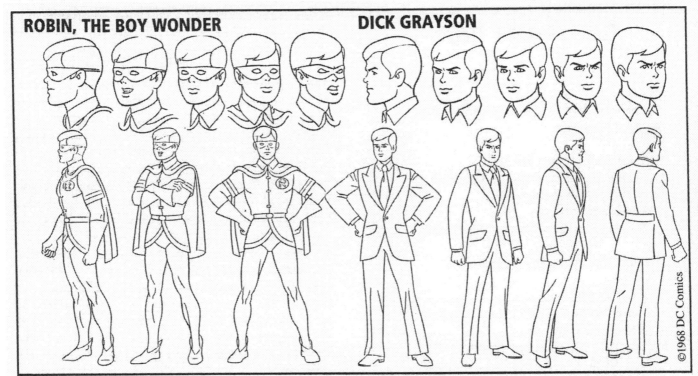

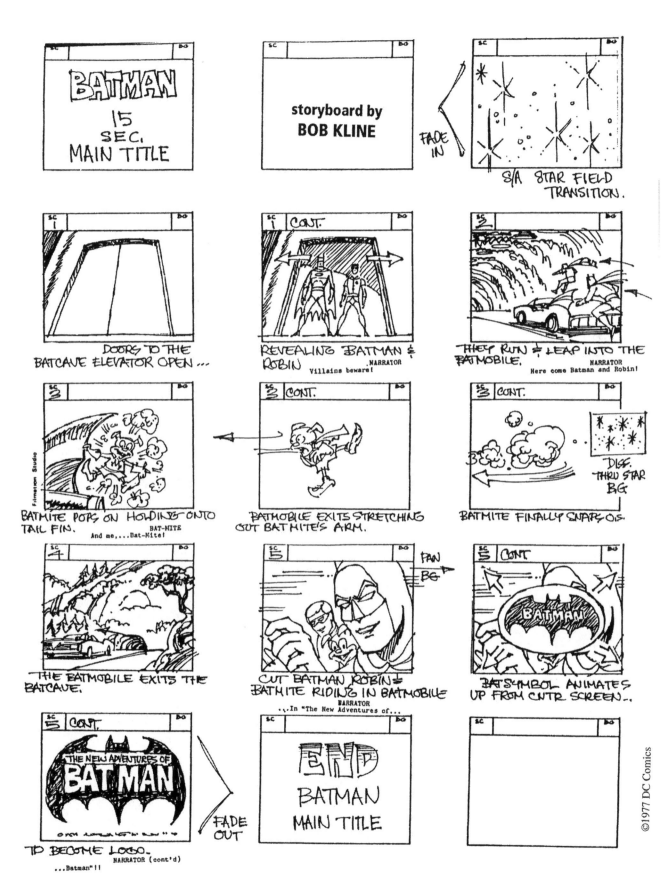

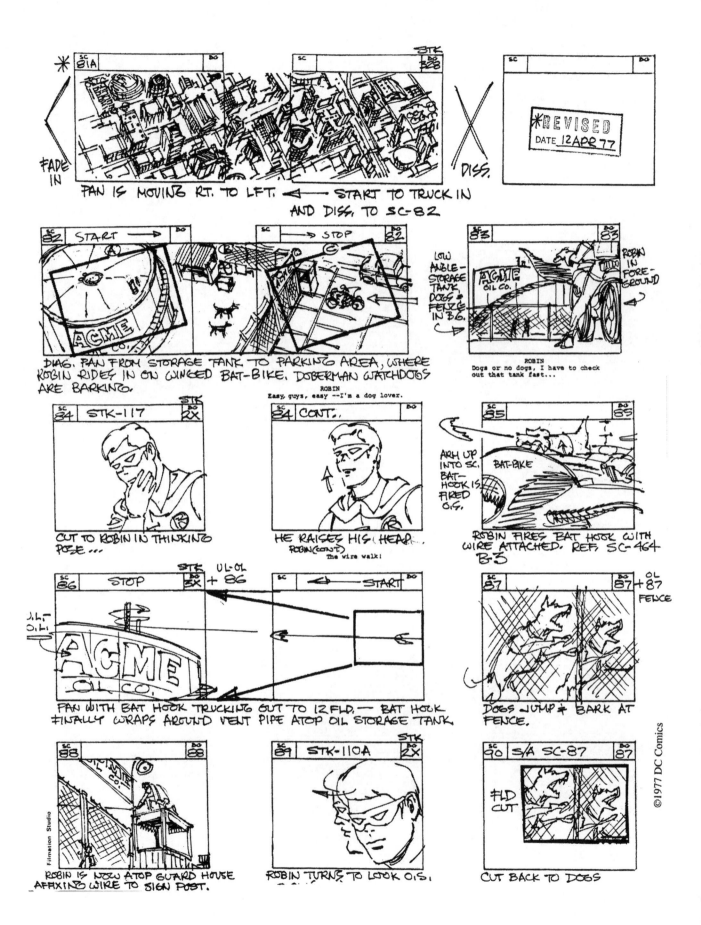

BLACKSTAR

Broadcast History:
Network Premiere: CBS, September, 1981
Saturday Mornings
Syndication Premiere: September, 1985

Executive Producers: Norm Prescott, Lou Scheimer
Producer: Don Christenson
Story Editor: Tom Ruegger

Principal Characters and Voices:
BLACKSTAR..George DiCenzo
GOSSAMEAR / BURBLE / RIF...........................Frank Welker
CARPO / OVERLORD.................................Alan Oppenheimer
BALKAR / TERRA / KLONE ....Pat Pinney
MARA..Linda Gary

Astronaut John Blackstar, lost in an alien universe, is rescued by the tiny Trobbit people. He joins their fight for freedom against the tyrannical evil of the Overlord. Assisted by Mara, the sorceress, and "Spock-like" Klone, who has the power to transform himself into any living being, Blackstar rides atop his flying dragon, Warlock, and uses the magical Starsword to challenge the Overlord's evil forces, as well as his own Starsword.

After ABC's success with Ruby-Spears' *Thundarr the Barbarian* series in 1980, fantasy once again became a viable creative option for Saturday morning animated series, with the other two networks seeking to jump on the bandwagon.

Filmation, riding high on its reputation as the premiere action-adventure animation production house, became CBS's primary animation supplier that season by adding this series to their new schedule along with the new *Zorro* and the returning *Tarzan, Lone Ranger, and Super 7 series*... but not without a few problems from the network.

The Blackstar series was presented to CBS as the first black superhero, action-adventure, animated series. The network was sure that middle America was not ready for this type of show with a black star, therefore, the models were changed into this "safe" cartoon with *Blackstar* becoming the white hero of the series. The Trobbits were at first just three small creatures, fashioned after the "Morlocks" from the movie *The Time Machine*. The network again thought America was not ready for this type of monster as a hero, and someone at the network thought it might be better if they were cuter; CBS liked the number seven, after Walt Dinsey's *Snow White*, so Filmation changed the three to seven, their skin color from blue to pink, and added seven different personalities.

Even though only thirteen episodes were produced and the show ran for only a single season, it enjoyed a brief rebirth in syndicated weekly reruns. But Blackstar's impact on Filmation's fortunes was bigger than anyone at the studio could ever imagine, for it was the Blackstar series that convinced toymaker Mattel that the studio would be ideal to produce an animated cartoon based on a new toy they were going to introduce in 1983. That cartoon was *He-Man and the Masters* of the Universe, which changed for all time the way television animation was produced. Also ironic was the fact that several years after the "*He-Man*" toy-line became a hit, a rival toy company licensed and created a line of Blackstar action figures which led to the series' brief syndicated revival...thus for a while making a rival in the toy business of the character that brought Mattel to Filmation in the first place.

BLACKSTAR
☐ SEARCH FOR THE STARSWORD
☐ THE CITY OF THE ANCIENT ONES
☐ THE LORD OF TIME
☐ THE MERMAID OF SERPENT SEA
☐ THE QUEST
☐ SPACEWRECKED
☐ LIGHTNING CITY OF THE CLOUDS
☐ KINGDOM OF NEPTUL
☐ TREE OF EVIL
☐ THE AIR WHALES OF ANCHAR

JOHN BLACKSTAR
An Earth Astronaut swept through a black hole. He becomes the hero of the planet Sagar and the little Trobbit people, both of whom are being menaced by the evil Overlord.

BALKAR / TERRA / CARPO / BURBLE / POULO / GOSSAMEAR / RIF

MARA
A lovely sorceress who aids the Trobbits in their struggle against villainy.

THE TROBBITS
The Trobbits all live in the fabulous Sagar tree. These elfin creatures symbolize the spirit of good on Sagar, a spirit that must always be strong to fight against the Overlord's villainy.

KLONE
A debonair alien hero who can take the shape of any living creature.

WARLOCK
Blackstar's flying dragon-like steed.

OVERLORD
This evil entity seeks to dominate all Sagar, and then the universe. He is villainy incarnate, possessing tremendous magic powers. The only ones who dare stand against him are Blackstar and his allies.

©1981 Filmation

Original presentation art for the CBS series by artist Bob Kline

- ☐ THE OVERLORD'S BIG SPELL
- ☐ THE CROWN OF THE SORCERESS
- ☐ THE ZOMBIE MASTER

☐ animation by FILMATION

THE BRADY KIDS

Broadcast History:
Network Premiere: ABC, September 1972, Saturday Mornings
Syndication Premiere: Fall 1979
Producers: Norm Prescott, Lou Scheimer
Director: Hal Sutherland
Writer: Marc Richards
Executive Consultant/Creator: Sherwood Schwartz

Principal Characters and Voices:
GREG BRADY ...Barry Williams (1972), Lane Scheimer (1973)
MARSHA BRADY..
..................Maureen McCormick (1972), Erica Scheimer (1973)
PETER BRADY..
.........................Christopher Knight (1972), Keith Allen (1973)
JAN BRADY..Eve Plumb
BOBBY BRADY.. Michael Lookinland
CINDY BRADY..Susan Olsen
MARLON / PING / PONG / FLEETWOOD........... Larry Storch
BABS.. Jane Webb
MOPTOP.."Lassie"

When ABC, then a perennial third-place finisher in the Saturday morning race to CBS and NBC, hit upon the idea of creating an animated spin-off of its highly-rated primetime sitcom, *The Brady Bunch*, it had no idea that the cartoon would become so well-received. In fact, the show's popularity lifted the network's Saturday morning schedule to within an arm's length of CBS and ahead of NBC in 1972. The show also inspired a "new series" trend.

ABC wanted to make Saturday mornings "primetime for kids" (this concept was also behind that season's *Saturday Superstar Movie*), hence: *The Brady Kids*, a cartoon starring six live-action "Bradys" vocalizing their animated counterparts. It was the success of this concept that set the standard for a subsequent flood of past and present TV series being adopted into animation. *Brady Bunch* creator Sherwood Schwartz, impressed by the fact that his children (along with some of the actual Bradys) loved Filmation's *Archie* series, personally selected Filmation to produce *The Brady Kids*...a show which definitely reflected its live-action predecessor in more than just attitude.

For example, when *The Brady Kids* sang their musical numbers in each episode, Filmation, in a prime reflection of their austere attitudes toward animated series, simply reworked their animation over previously-animated *Archie* stock footage: Greg re-animating Archie's guitar movements; Marsha re-animating Betty's tambourine motions; Bobby on Jughead's drums; Jan on Veronica's organ; and Peter on Reggie's guitar. Since there were only five members in the Archie band, new motions were animated for Cindy's guitar playing. The real irony, of course, was that Barry Williams, who played Greg, was the only Brady who could play a musical instrument (however, all of them sang their own songs and the group did record five albums). The Filmation "austere approach" continued as, to animate the Brady's dog Moptop, they reworked old animation of Jughead's dog Hot Dog, painting him brown and using Lassie's barks and growls (from the Lassie pilot they produced that season) for Moptop's vocals.

Visually, even though the kid's clubhouse was all-new, the town they lived in was basically composed of Archie's Riverdale backgrounds. At one point, they took the typical Saturday-morning animation convention of never changing the characters clothing to somewhat ridiculous extremes: the kids (who despite the difference in their ages [7-16] all went to the same school) play the championship high school football game (and lead in football cheers) in their street clothes!

Marc Richards, who single-handedly wrote every episode of the series, created the three pets that joined *The Brady Kids* along on their exploits: Ping and Pong, the Chinese-gibberish spouting panda bear astronauts, and Marlon, the magical talking mynah bird whose wrong-way mystical prowess got them into situations they would never get into on *The Brady Bunch* series. Introduced in a special hour-length episode that also kicked off ABC's *Saturday Superstar Movie*, Marlon's magic also precipitated the kids' run-ins with several animated super-hero guest stars (a testing process that eventually led to ABC's *Super Friends* the following season). Among those "heroes" were The

THE BRADY KIDS

Lone Ranger, Superman, Wonder Woman, and *Mission Magic's* Miss Tickle.

Filmation's austere (some might unkindly say "cheap") approach took another interesting turn the following season: when the show was renewed for another season, the three older Brady refused to voice the characters for the money offered. This led to Lou Scheimer recruiting his son, Lane, and daughter, Erica, to replace two of them. In another twist, Columbia, noting Paramount's success with its cartoon, tried to interest ABC in a possible animated version of the Brady Friday night companion, *The Partridge Family*. ABC refused, and Columbia took the concept to CBS whom, being pitched a new *Jetsons* series by Hanna-Barbera, combined the two to create *Partridge Family: 2200 A.D.* With only a third of the original voice talents of its parent show (and none of its singers), the cartoon lasted only thirty-two weeks on CBS in 1974—a mere fraction of *The Brady Kids* run on ABC.

THE BRADY KIDS 1972
- [ ] JUNGLE BUNGLE PART I -II
- [ ] DOUBLE TROUBLE
- [ ] LONE GONE SILVER
- [ ] CINDY'S SUPER FRIEND
- [ ] POP GOES THE MYNAH
- [ ] WHO WAS THAT DOG?
- [ ] IT AIN'T NECESSARILY SNOW
- [ ] A FUNNY THING HAPPENED ON THE WAY TO THE FOOTBALL FIELD
- [ ] THAT WAS NO WORTHY OPPONENT, THAT WAS MY SISTER
- [ ] YOU TOOK THE WORDS RIGHT OUT OF MY TAPE
- [ ] GIVE ME A HOME WHERE THE PANDA BEARS ROAM
- [ ] IT'S ALL GREEK TO ME
- [ ] THE BIG TIME
- [ ] THE BIRTHDAY PARTY
- [ ] THE RICHEST MAN IN THE WORLD WINS

1973
- [ ] FRANKINCENSE
- [ ] TEACHER'S PET
- [ ] MARCIA'S LIB
- [ ] CEILING ZERO
- [ ] WHO BELIEVES IN GHOSTS

BRAVESTARR

Broadcast History:
Syndication Premiere: Fall 1988

Executive Producer: Lou Scheimer
Executive in Charge of Production: Arthur Nadel
Series Writer / Developer: Bob Forward
Art Director: John Grusd
Director: Marsh LaMore, Lou Kachivas, Ed Friedman, Lou Zukor
Feature Directors: Bob Arkwright

Principal Characters and Voices:
MARSHALL BRAVESTARR .... Pat Fraley

BRAVESTARR

THRITY-THRITY

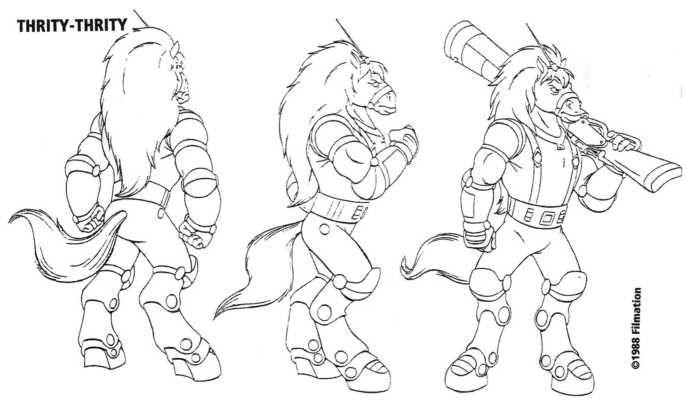

©1988 Filmation

OUTLAW SCUZZ / DEPUTY FUZZ .... Charles Adler
TEX HEX / STAMPEDE .... Alan Oppenheier
THRITY-THRITY / SHAMAN .... Ed Gilbert
JUDGE J.B. .... Susan Blu

When Filmation bowed out of series production in 1988 at least they left with a bang for, while most studios level of quality in their production tended to worsen towards the end, Filmation last series, *Bravestatrr*, was almost at the level of their previous high-water mark, *The New Adventures of Flash Gordon*. Part of this may have been due to a similarity in their production methods, as much of the animation in both series was based on stock animation originally produced for feature versions of both series, with budgets to match.

Actually the genesis for what was to become *Bravestarr* begin three seasons earlier in 1984, during the development process being engaged on the animated *Ghostbustes*. The *Bravestarr* series main adversary was Tex Hex, originally conceived to serve as a ghostly ally to the *Ghostbusters'* main villain, Prime Evil. Lou Scheimer, noting him during the development process, pulled Tex Hex from further consideration and asked Head Writer, Arthur Nadel and Art Director, John Grusd to develop another possible concept around him.

The concept that was later conceived was summarized by Scheimer as "cowboys and aliens", or in other words a "space western", centering on the inhabitants of the planet New Texas, set in the year 2349 during a "Kerium (their version of gold) rush". Underneath the planet's pink sky and its three moons, the inhabitants play out scenarios reminiscent of those that took place in the Wild West of the 1800's. of earth. Bravestarr with the help of his friends Thirty-Thirty, the robot/horse and Judge J.B., protected the Prairie People and citizens of New Texas against the outlaw Tex Hex and his outlaw group.

Once the main characters and concepts were developed, Filmation took the bible and storyboards to Mattel Toys for a possible licensing / co-production deal. Mindful of the facts that Mattel had utilized the services of other animation companies to produce their properties beside Filmation, and Mattel had turned down the opportunity to license their Ghostbusters for action figures the previous year. Filmation asked for and got a better licensing deal with Bravestarr, than with either *He-Man and the Masters of the Universe* or *She-Ra, Princess of Power*. Filmation having brought them the property, served as more creative partners on the deal. After two years of the usual creative wrangling over points minor (Filmation wanted Bravestarr to wear a gold costume, Mattel, fearing boys would not buy a "sissy"" color like gold wanted blue, the two opting for a mixture of both) and major, (Bravestarr and the mystic powers he can summon are both based on Indian ancestry, the former were ignored and the latter tamed down in Mattel's presentation of the conceit). The Bravestarr toys made their debut in Christmas of 1986, nine months before the animated series made its debut. Three months before, a similar animated "space cowboy" syndicated series, *Adventures of the Galaxy Rangers* had made it's debut… to dismal ratings. With a lack of a corresponding toy line seen as part of the reason for its failure. Bravestarr had the toy line, (itself part of the high-tech laser technology symbolized by the very popular "Laser Tag" toys). Mattel's marketing muscle and the lines early rollout to ensure its success.

By early spring the "infrared technology / Lazer Tag" toy was already showing signs of sputtering popularity as far as kids were concerned. By summer of 1987, the Laser Tag and Bravestarr toy were already starting to collect dust on the store half-price shelves. Not a good sign for a series that had yet to debut. Work proceeded on both the series, to air that fall, and the origin feature, *Bavestarr the Legend,* which was to premiere that Christmas. The series had to overcome early resistance to use on gunplay in the episodes delivered overall some of the harder, content-wise, Filmation stories since *The New Adventures of Flash Gordon*, particularly in the episode "The Price", a futuristic drug abuse parable in which the lead character, a twelve year-old "Spin" user, actually died in the end of the story, thus driving home the usual Filmation moral in a particularly hard-hitting fashion.

Despite the overall high production quality of the series, the failure of the toy line and low ratings generated by the series itself, compounded by its high production costs due to Lou Scheimer's determination of keeping all production in the U.S., rather than shipping the majority of it overseas. The series resigned to a lingering over-the-air doom during the '87 - '88 season. The *Bravestarr* feature was sent to the limbo of unreleased films, where few people to this day have actually seen it.

Filmation's hopes for the series' success were so high that the studio produced two segments that were meant to spin off future series for the company. In one of the planned spin-offs,

THIRTY-THRITY'S TRANSFORMATION

Sherlock Holmes in the 23th Century, the legendary sleuth created by Sir Arthur Conan Doyle fell into a time warp and ended up in Bravestarr's time and planet where he encountered not only Bravestarr, but his old adversary Professor Morrarity in the two-part story which was incorporated into the series. Produced separately from the series was Bravo, a spin-off starring the impish Pairie People, relatives of Bravestarr characters Scuzz and Fuzz and their comical misadventures. This series had gone so far as to have had many episodes scripted, storyboarded and in the layout stage when new owners L'orel pulled the plug on studio operations in 1988, just when the studio had decided to finally send some of the production overseas to cut down on cost.

BRAVESTARR
- [ ] NEW TEXAS BLUES
- [ ] NIGHT OF THE BRONCOTANK
- [ ] THE POWER WITHIN
- [ ] SPACE ZOO
- [ ] BROTHER'S KEEPER
- [ ] KERIUM FEVER
- [ ] THE TAKING OF THISTLEDOWN 123
- [ ] NO DRUMS, NO TRUMPETS
- [ ] SHOWDOWN AT SAWTOOTH
- [ ] BRAVESTARR AND THE LAW
- [ ] EYE OF THE BEHOLDER
- [ ] NOMAD IS AN ISLAND
- [ ] THE BALLAD OF SARA JANE
- [ ] EYEWITNESS
- [ ] BRAVESTARR AND THE MEDALLION
- [ ] THE PRICE
- [ ] HAIL, HAIL, THE GANG'S ALL HERE
- [ ] THOREN THE SLAVEMASTER
- [ ] TO WALK A MILE
- [ ] SCUZZ AND FUZZ
- [ ] WHO AM I?
- [ ] THE VIGILANTES
- [ ] THE WITNESSES
- [ ] THE WRONG HANDS
- [ ] THE GOOD, THE BAD, AND THE CLUMSY
- [ ] WILD CHILD
- [ ] JEREMIAH AND THE PRAIRIE PEOPLE
- [ ] UNSUNG HERO
- [ ] AN OLDER HAND
- [ ] HOSTAGE
- [ ] RUNAWAY PLANET
- [ ] BRAVESTARR AND THE TREATY
- [ ] LOST MOUNTAIN
- [ ] HANDLEBAR AND RAMPAGE
- [ ] HAUNTED SHIELD
- [ ] FALLEN IDOL
- [ ] BIG THIRTY AND LITTLE WIMBLE
- [ ] MEMORIES
- [ ] BUDDY
- [ ] RAMPAGE!
- [ ] NEW TEXAS BLUES
- [ ] NIGHT OF THE BRONCOTANK

- ☐ THE POWER WITHIN
- ☐ SPACE ZOO
- ☐ BROTHER'S KEEPER
- ☐ KERIUM FEVER
- ☐ THE TAKING OF THISTLEDOWN 123
- ☐ NO DRUMS, NO TRUMPETS
- ☐ SHOWDOWN AT SAWTOOTH
- ☐ BRAVESTARR AND THE LAW
- ☐ EYE OF THE BEHOLDER
- ☐ NOMAD IS AN ISLAND
- ☐ THE BALLAD OF SARA JANE
- ☐ EYEWITNESS
- ☐ BRAVESTARR AND THE MEDALLION
- ☐ HAIL, HAIL, THE GANG'S ALL HERE
- ☐ THOREN THE SLAVEMASTER
- ☐ TO WALK A MILE
- ☐ SCUZZ AND FUZZ
- ☐ WHO AM I?
- ☐ SHERLOCK HOLMES IN THE 23RD CENTURY PART I - II

FABULOUS FUNNIES

*(also know as **ARCHIE'S TV FUNNIES**)*

Broadcast History:
Network Premiere: NBC, September, 1978 Saturday Mornings

Executive Producers: Norm Prescott, Lou Scheimer
Producer: Don Christensen
Directors: Ed Friedman, Marsh La More, Gwen Wetzler, Kay

Wright, Lou Zukor
Writers: Jim Ryan, Bill Danch, Sam Simon, Buzz Dixon

Principal Characters and Voices:
BROOM HILDA / SLUGGO / OOLA / HANS AND FRITZ
KATZENJAMMER...June Foray
NANCY / EMMY LOU ....Jayne Hamil
GAYLORD / ALLY OOP / FOOZY / CAPTAIN
KATZENJAMMER .... Bob Holt
TUMBLEWEEDS / IRWIN / INSPECTOR / KING GUZZLE /
GRELBER ....Alan Oppenheimer

Seeking to duplicate the ratings success of its 1971 CBS series *Archie's TV Funnies,* Filmation licensed many of the same animated segments for the same boss, Fred Silverman, at a different network, NBC. *The Fabulous Funnies* re-introduced "TV Funnies" character Broom Hilda, the abrasive-natured witch, spellmaker, and endearing character who used her powers to satisfy whims and peeves more than to terrorize. The episodes included her comics' coterie: Gaylord, the intellectual buzzard that seldom heeded her commands; Irwin, the shy and shaggy troll; and the insolent Grebler, the master of insult, who lives in a log. Alley Oop possessed Herculean strength and over-sized forearms which resembled those of the salty seaman, Popeye. The prehistoric muscleman rode a pet dinosaur named Dinny and brought order to the Kingdom of Moo, ruled by King Guzzle, his treacherous Grand Vizier Foozy, and Queen Umpateedle. The Captain and the Kids, Hans and Fritz, continued their pranks at the expense of their long-suffering Mama and the irascible Captain Katzenjammer. They were modeled on German cartoonist Wilhelm Busch's nineteenth-century destructive brats, Max and Moritz, a pair of young miscreants. Nancy, a precocious young-

ster who made her debut in the twenties as the niece of Fritzi Ritz was paired with the pseudo-tough Sluggo. Alley Oop was brought to network television by NBC programming head Fred Silverman and featured a tribe of comical cavemen. Silverman felt so strongly that the "original" Flintstones cartoon series (the comic strip predated *The Flintstones* by some 30 years) would be a ratings magnet for the show that he made one of the characters in the strip, "Fozzy," the series' host. Emphasizing Filmation's pro-educational stance, each half hour of the series focused on a particular pro-social topic. Some of these had not been previously dealt with on a Saturday morning kid's cartoon show. Two of those segments won awards for the studio. The segments dealing with Broom Hilda's drinking problem and the touching episode dealing with death and how it affected the Alley Oop cast.

A tried-and-true comics' concept that sacrificed much of its humor and fun for preaching, *The Fabulous Funnies* lost the ratings race after one year to its more entertaining competition.

With the exception of Alley Oop and Tumbleweeds, all of the shows previously appeared on *Archie's TV Funnies*, but none of the *TV Funnies*' segments were used. *Tumbleweeds* only aired on the first episode.

*(**Author's Note:** Tumbleweeds, based on Tom K. Ryan's western comic strip, only made a single appearance on the series. Filmation never received the rights to use the characters, a fact that no one at the studio knew until Ryan called the network the Monday after the first and only appearance of* Tumbleweeds. *Needless to say, the matter was quickly settled, and the strip made no further appearances. However, the one aired episode did make it to video on* The Fabulous Funnies, Volume 1*)*

FABULOUS FUNNIES
- ANIMAL CRACK-UPS
- SCHOOL DAZE
- COMIC-ITION
- BODS AND CLODS
- SAVE OUR WORLD
- BUT, WOULD YOU WANT YOUR SISTER TO MARRY AN ARTIST?
- MONEY MADNESS
- FEAR
- DIFFERENT JOKES FOR DIFFERENT FOLKS
- DEATH
- SAFETY SECOND
- DRINKING
- SHOT IN THE LIGHT

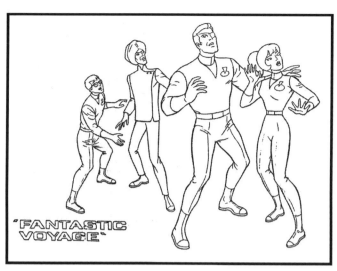
"FANTASTIC VOYAGE"

FANTASTIC VOYAGE

Broadcast History:
Network Premiere: ABC, September, 1968, Saturday Mornings

Syndicated History:
Cable Premiere: Sci-Fi Channel, October 1992
Executive Producers: Louis Scheimer, Norman Prescott
Director: Hal Sutherland
Story Editor: Ken Sobel

Principal Characters and Voices:
COMMANDER JONATHAN KIDD / PROF. CARTER...............
....Ted Knight
ERICA LANE............…..........…..........................Jane Webb
BUSBY BIRDWELL / GURU..............................Marvin Miller

With the rating's success of *Journey to the Center of the Earth*, produced for the ABC network the previous season and based on a 20th Century Fox live-action feature, the network then asked Filmation for another animated series based on yet another 20th Century Fox sci-fi/adventure feature. The one decided on was one based on the then-hit movie *Fantastic Voyage*, which starred Stephen Boyd and Raquel Welch, and detailed the adventures of a team of scientists aboard the nuclear-powered submarine, Proteus. The characters were atomically-miniaturized to the size of microbes and injected into the bloodstream of a noted scientist who was smuggled from behind the Iron Curtain and during his escape incurred a serious brain injury. In a race against death, they encountered a variety of biological dangers on their way to destroying a deadly aneurysm that threatened his life.

The animated series took the movie concept several steps further with a secret government agency being formed for the purposes of espionage activities against those who sought to undermine America during the height of the Cold War. This agency, the Combined Miniature Defense Force (C. M. D. F.), possessed the high-tech ability to shrink humans with the ultimate goal of fielding a select group of adventurers as a microscopic, "Mission: Impossible" style team to undertake perilous spy missions. This team was composed of leader Commander Jonathan Kidd, biologist Erica Lane, abrasive Voyager creator/pilot, Busby Birdwell, and the Mr. Spock-like, Guru, a master of mysterious mystic powers. During their trips, the task force was challenged by missions that took them from far away enemy countries to the deepest recesses of outer space. Their exploits were made all the more perilous by the shrinking machine's one drawback…a twelve-hour limit to the time the team could stay miniaturized.

(*Author's Note:* Lou Scheimer came up with the name of Erica Lane after his daughter Erica and his son Lane. Also, Science Fiction writer, Issac Asimov, wrote the novelization of this premise)

FANTASTIC VOYAGE
☐ THE GATHERING OF THE TEAM
☐ THE MENACE FROM SPACE
☐ THE MAGIC CRYSTAL OF KABALA
☐ THE ATOMIC INVADERS
☐ THE MASTER SPY
☐ THE MIND OF THE MASTER
☐ GONE TODAY, HERE TOMORROW
☐ THE DAY THE FOOD DISAPPEARED
☐ REVENGE OF THE SPY
☐ THE HOBBY HOUSE
☐ THE GREAT BUSBY
☐ THE SPY SATELLITE
☐ FIRST MEN ON THE MOON
☐ THE BARNACLE BOMBS
☐ THE PERFECT CRIME
☐ THE WORLD'S FAIR AFFAIR
☐ THE MOST DANGEROUS GAME

FAT ALBERT | BILL COSBY | BUCKY | DUMB DONALD | RUSSELL | WEIRD HAROLD | RUDY | MUSHMOUTH

FAT ALBERT AND THE COSBY KIDS

Broadcast History:
FAT ALBERT AND THE COSBY KIDS
Network Premiere: CBS, September, 1972, Saturday Mornings

THE NEW FAT ALBERT SHOW (with THE BROWN HORNET)
Network Premiere: CBS, September, 1979 Saturday Mornings

BILL COSBY'S FAT ALBERT AND THE COSBY KIDS
Syndication Premiere: Fall, 1985

Cable Premiere:
USA Network Fall, 1989

Executive Producer: Dr. William H. Cosby, Jr., pH.
Producers: Louis Scheimer, Norman Prescott
Directors: Don Christensen, Hal Sutherland, Don Towsley, Lou Zukor

Live Action Host..Bill Cosby
Live action Director .... Robert F. Chenault

Principal Characters and Voices:
FAT ALBERT / MUSHMOUTH / BILL / MUDFOOT / DUMB DONALD / BROWN HORNET.............................…....Bill Cosby
RUSSELL / BUCKY ....Eric Suter
WEIRD HAROLD ....Gerald Edwards
RUDY ....Jan Crawford

STINGER / LEGAL EAGLE ....Lou Scheimer

Fat Albert and The Cosby Kids were a band of north Philadelphia young black chums, derived from the wry memory and comic imagination of comedian Bill Cosby's childhood years in a Depression-era neighborhood. The unlikely hero was Fat Albert, a sloppy, rotund peacemaker whose favorite expression was, "Hey, hey, hey." He provided the example for working out the group's difficulties and problems. Among his pals were the tall and gangly Old Weird Harold, the oafish Dumb Donald, Rudy the Rich Kid, easy-going Bucky, the unintelligible Mushmouth, and tag-a-long Russell, modeled after Bill Cosby's younger brother. Cosby acted as host for the cartoons, and through his narration he underscored each program's theme and reinforced the lesson that the gang experienced.

Responding to mounting criticism over exploitive children's programming, Cosby pioneered the use of humor and entertainment in this animated format to instruct young people in social and ethical behavior. Designed for affective learning, the series dealt with such intangibles as influencing feelings, behavior, and value judgment. The stories emphasized such peer-group problems as the show-off and braggart, the child who lied to impress others, and the larger child who exploited little tots. The plots also dealt with such daily challenges as frustration, getting attention, understanding and accepting differences between persons, playing hookey, creativity, and personal courage... or the lack of it. In 1979-1980, *The New Fat Albert Show* took the friends from their salvage yard setting and bused them to school in another part of town where they encountered different life styles, experiences, and new problems to solve. Introduced in a cartoon show within the premise, "The Brown Hornet," a masked do-gooder with the tenacity of Superman and the finesse of Inspector Clouseau, appeared in brief adventures to help the gang solve some of their problems. The films were created under the supervision of a panel of scholars and educators including Dr. Gordon L. Berry of UCLA

The series was spurred by its reception to a half-hour prime time NBC Special produced by De-Patie/Freling, *Hey, Hey, Hey, It's Fat Albert* (Nov., 1969), in which the "Tackle Football Championship of the World" was at stake. Subsequently, the Cosby characters appeared in a go-cart race on NBC in Weird Harold (May, 1973), called because of CBS' ownership of the "Fat Albert" title and a pair of CBS thirty-minute programs featuring the do's and don'ts of trick-or-treating on *The Fat Albert Halloween Special* (Oct., 1977) and *The Fat Albert Christmas Special* (Dec., 1977).

Lauded for its attitude and content, *Fat Albert* demonstrated that an educational-message show could be commercially competitive. Acclaimed also as a landmark series in minority programming, *Fat Albert* was actually the third animated program featuring principally a black cast. Predecessors were *The Harlem Globetrotters* and ABC's *The Jackson 5ive*. The second longest-running cartoon show on the CBS Saturday schedule, behind *The Bugs Bunny Show*, in its ninth season in 1980-1981, *Fat Albert* was a grand high point, encompassing proven educational and social value among the network children's programs.

Unfortunately, while it was almost universally acclaimed among educators and parents, it was that acclaim more than the series' ratings that kept it on the air all those seasons. A fact made painfully apparent when Filmation decided to release the series in syndication with 50 newly-produced half-hours. Adding a new cartoon short to alternate with "The Brown Hornet", "The Legal Eagle" used a southern-fried sheriff eagle and his squirrel sidekick to teach kids the final points of law. This mix of old and new episodes garnered some of the worst ratings syndication animation had seen up to that time, but did lead to the series being picked up by the USA Cable network for broadcast in fall of 1989.

FAT ALBERT AND THE COSBY KIDS 1972
☐ LYING
☐ THE RUNT
☐ THE STRANGER
☐ CREATIVITY
☐ FISH OUT OF WATER
☐ MOVING
☐ PLAYING HOOKEY
☐ THE HOSPITAL
☐ BEGGING BENNY
☐ THE HERO
☐ THE PRANKSTER

1973
☐ MISTER BIG TIMER
☐ THE NEWCOMER
☐ WHAT DOES DAD DO?
☐ MOM OR POP?
☐ HOW THE WEST WAS LOST
☐ SIGN OFF

1975
☐ THE FUZZ
☐ OUNCE OF PREVENTION

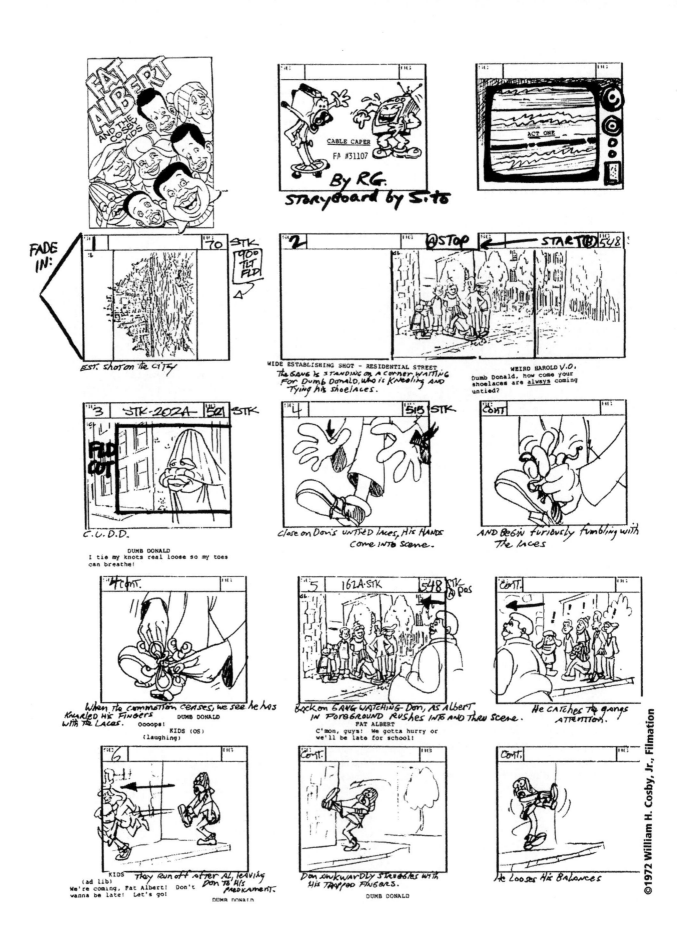

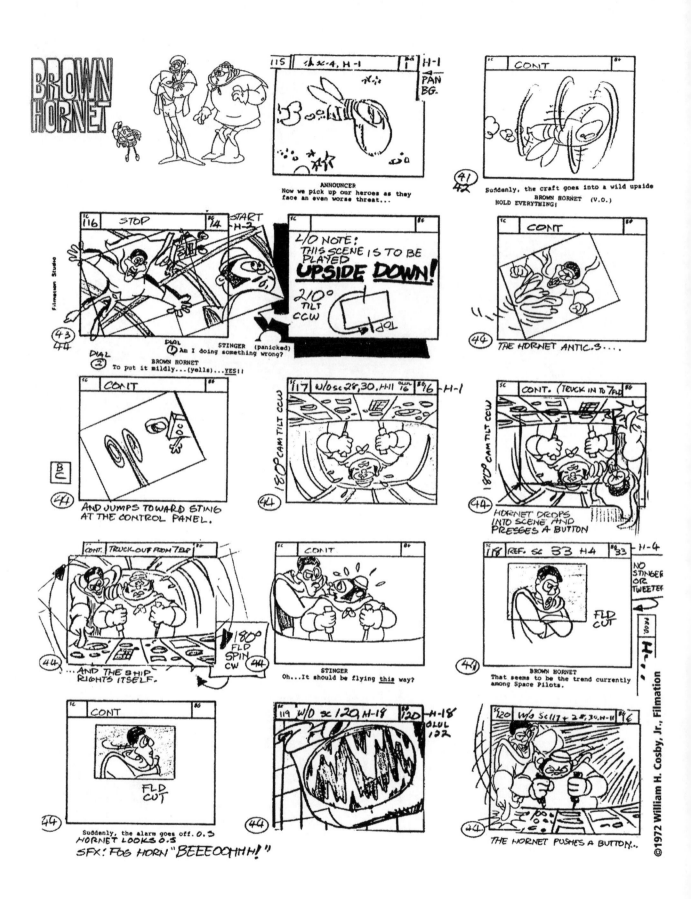

- ☐ FREE RIDE
- ☐ SOFT CORE

1980
- ☐ PAIN, PAIN GO AWAY
- ☐ THE RAINBOW
- ☐ THE SECRET
- ☐ EASY PICKINS
- ☐ GOOD OL' DUDES
- ☐ HEADS OR TAILS
- ☐ POT OF GOLD
- ☐ THE GUNSLINGER

1981
- ☐ HABLA ESPANOL
- ☐ THE FATHER
- ☐ TWO BY TWO
- ☐ DOUBLE CROSS
- ☐ BARKING DOG
- ☐ LITTLE GIRL FOUND
- ☐ WATER ARE YOU WATING FOR?
- ☐ WATCH THAT FIRST STEP

PRIME-TIME SPECIALS
- ☐ FAT ALBERT: THE GREAT GO-CART RACE
- ☐ FAT ALBERT EASTER SPECIAL
- ☐ FAT ALBERT HALLOWEEN SPECIAL
- ☐ FAT ALBERT CHRISTMAS SPECIAL

- ☐ FAT ALBERT MEETS DAN CUPID
- ☐ TAKE TWO, THEY'RE SMALL
- ☐ THE ANIMAL LOVER
- ☐ LITTLE TOUGH GUY

1976
- ☐ SMOKE GETS IN YOUR HAIR
- ☐ WHAT SAY?
- ☐ READIN', RITIN', AND RUDY SUEDE SIMPSON
- ☐ LITTLE BUSINESS
- ☐ TV OR NOT TV
- ☐ THE SHUTTERED WINDOW
- ☐ JUNK FOOD

1979 (with the Brown Hornet)
- ☐ IN MY MERRY BUSMOBLIE
- ☐ THE DANCER
- ☐ SPARE THE ROD
- ☐ SWEET SORROW
- ☐ POLL TIME
- ☐ THE MAINSTREAM

Flash Gordon

THE NEW ADVENTURES OF FLASH GORDON

Broadcast History
Network Premiere: NBC, September, 1979 Saturday Mornings (with a two-hour primetime animated movie)

Producers: Lou Scheimer, Norm Prescott
Producer: Don Christensen
Directors: Hal Sutherland, Don Towsley, Lou Zukor

Principal Characters and Voices
FLASH GORDON / PRINCE BARON.................Robert Ridgely
DALE ARDEN ....Diane Pershing
DR. HANS ZARKOV / MING THE MERCILESS......................
………….......……..................……..........Alan Oppenheimer
PRINCESS AURA / QUEEN FRIA……...…….....Melendy Britt
THUN / VULTAN….............................. Alan Melvin / Ted Cassidy
GREMLIN ..…….......….....................……..........Lou Scheimer

With the successful return of heroic action to Saturday morning television, spearheaded by ABC's Superfriends and CBS's *Tarzan and the Super 7*, all the major animation studios sought out more adventure heroes to bring to the small screen. Flash Gordon was one of producer/creative director Don Christensen's favorite comics and, assembling a small army of Filmation's finest artists to the task, he was already at work on a two-hour animated feature version of Flash for NBC. At the same time, famed film producer Dino De Laurentis was producing a big-budget, live-action version of the Alex Raymond strip. Rather than regard the animated version as competition for his project, De Laurentis was in fact so impressed with Filmation's work-in-progress that when the studio started running into budget problems on Flash, he invested some of his own money into the animated film.

Less campy and more faithful to the comic strip than De Laurentis' version, the movie-in-progress boasted a well-written script by sci-fi veteran Samuel A. Peeples as well as great voice performances by Robert Ridgely and the last vocal performance by Ted Cassidy, "Lurch" of television's *The Addams Family*. NBC was impressed enough with the animation quality, due in part to heavy use of rotoscoping, to commission an animated series utilizing the feature's animation to create extensive "stock footage" to build the episodes around. Dismal ratings for the series' first season caused NBC to renew the series for a second season with changes to bring in more of a younger viewing crowd. Filmation attempted to do this by lightening up the scripts and giving Flash a little baby dragon named Gremlin for a pet. This change did not work for the many viewer the series captured its first season, which ranked quality-wise with the original Jonny Quest in terms of adult appeal. With poorer ratings, the series was ended in 1981.

FLASH GORDON
☐ CHAPTER ONE : A PLANET IN PERIL
☐ CHAPTER TWO: THE MONSTERS OF MONGO
☐ CHAPTER THREE: VULTAN, KING OF THE HAWKMEN
☐ CHAPTER FOUR: TO SAVE EARTH
☐ CHAPTER FIVE: THE BEAST MEN'S PREY
☐ CHAPTER SIX: INTO THE WATER
☐ CHAPTER SEVEN: ADVENTURE IN ARBORIA
☐ CHAPTER EIGHT: THE FROZEN WORLD
☐ CHAPTER NINE: MONSTER OF GLACIER
☐ CHAPTER TEN: BLUE MAGIC
☐ CHAPTER ELEVEN: KING FLASH!
☐ CHAPTER TWELVE: MING'S TOURNAMENT OF DEATH
☐ CHAPTER THIRTEEN: CASTAWAYS IN TROPICA
☐ CHAPTER FOURTEEN: THE DESERT HAWK
☐ CHAPTER FIFTEEN: REVOLT OF THE POWER MEN
☐ CHAPTER SIXTEEN: MING'S LAST BATTLE

© 1978 King Features Syndicate, Inc.

Ming the Merciless

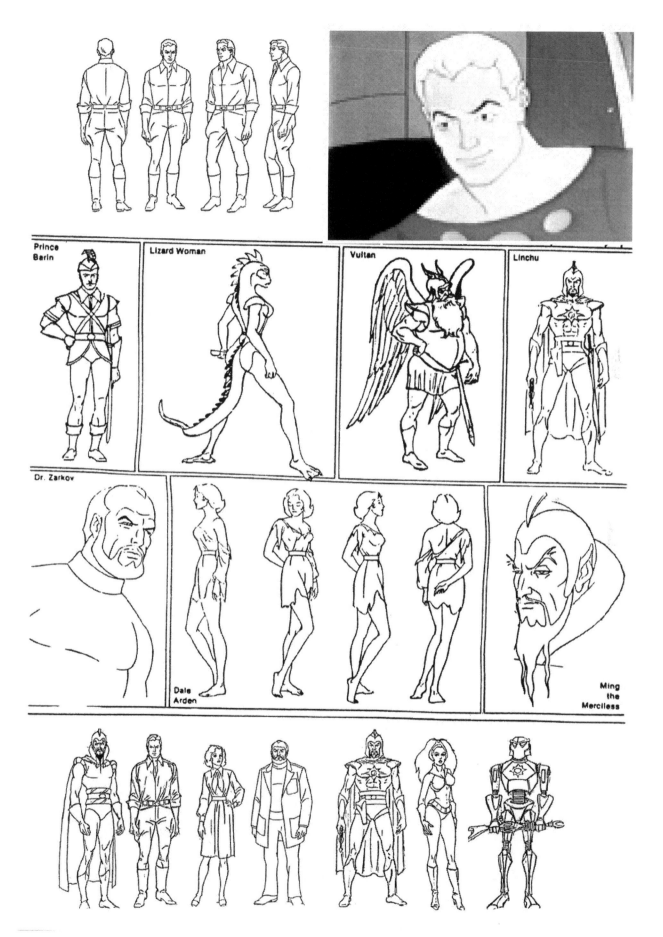

NOTE: SC-19 IS A MASTER SHOT. SCENES 22, 24, 26, 29C, 34, 41 ALL W/O OF SC-19.

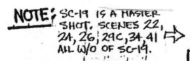

| SC 19 | FLASH'S P.O.V. — UPSHOT OF DRAGON HOLDING DALE | BG 19 |

— MAKE THIS BG A 2 FLD PAN.

SC 18 | C.U. - FLASH | BG 18

FLASH REACTS IN HORROR TO WHAT HE SEES. CAM TRUCKS IN FAST.

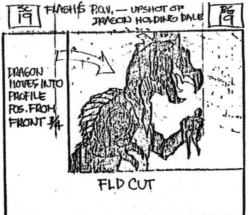

DRAGON MOVES INTO PROFILE POS. FROM FRONT 3/4

FLD CUT

DRAGON EXAMINES DALE FOR A MOMENT, TURNING HIS HAND & COCKING HIS HEAD FROM SIDE TO SIDE.

SC 19 CONT.

THE DRAGON TURNS & STEPS AWAY FROM CAM. CARRYING DALE IN IT'S LEFT CLAW.
NOTE: DRAGON TAKES ONLY ONE OR TWO STEPS THEN CUT.

SFX: LOUD HISSING & SNORTING

SC 20 | L.S. LOW ANGLE — INCLUDE ROCKET, FLASH & DRAGON | BG 20

THE DRAGON MOVES DIAGONALLY PAST CAM. AS THE TINY FIGURE OF FLASH CLIMBS OUT ONTO THE BENT OVER FLAP OF THE SHIP'S...

SC 21

FLASH FINISHES STANDING UP...

SC 21 CONT.

— ROCKET

HE RAISES THE RIFLE & FIRES

SFX: BANG

⑥

SC 22 | W/O SC-19 | BG 19

CLOSE ON DRAGON AS HE WHIPS AROUND TO ROAR AT FLASH.

ROAR!!

SC 23 | L.S. ZARKOV'S SHIP FRAMES SCENE. | BG 22

THE DRAGON TURNS AROUND & BACKS UP A FEW STEPS. FLASH SHIFTS HIS WEIGHT & LOWERS HIS RIFLE. ZARKOV APPEARS AT THE HOLE IN THE SHIP'S HULL.

SC 23 CONT.

DECIDING FLASH IS NOT A THREAT THE DRAGON TURNS AWAY AND CONCENTRATES ON DALE

NOTE: KEEP DRAGONS' TAILS ACTIVE DURING THIS ENTIRE SEQUENCE.

(1980 12-minute episodes)
- ☐ BEWARE OF GIFTS
- ☐ GREMLIN THE DRAGON
- ☐ ROYAL WEDDING
- ☐ SIR GREMLIN
- ☐ DEADLY DOUBLE
- ☐ THE GAME
- ☐ WITCH WOMAN
- ☐ THE WARRIOR
- ☐ THE FREEDOM BALLOON
- ☐ THE SEED
- ☐ GREMLIN'S FINEST HOUR
- ☐ MICRO MENACE
- ☐ THE SURVIVAL GAME
- ☐ FLASH BACK
- ☐ THE MEMORY BANK OF MING
- ☐ SACRIFICE OF THE VOLCANO MEN

THE GHOST BUSTERS
(the animated series)

Broadcast History:
Syndication Premiere:- September, 1986

Executive Producer: Lou Scheimer

Principal Characters:
JAKE KONG JR.	Pat Fraley
EDDIE SPENCER JR.	Peter Cullen
PRIME EVIL	Alan Oppenheimer
FUTURA	Susan Blu
JESSICA	Linda Gary
G.B. HAUNTER.	Erik Gunden
JESSICA'S NEPHEW	Erika Scheimer
TRACY	Lou Scheimer

When Columbia Pictures produced the multi-million grossing comedy *Ghostbusters*, they made a slight mistake...they neglected the fact that Filmation had produced a live-action comedy series with the same name for CBS in 1975. Filmation sued the studio in 1985 and, without revealing the terms of the out-of-court settlement, made a mistake of their own, as Lou Scheimer had admitted: "We should have asked for the animation rights for their (Columbia's) *Ghostbusters* as part of the settlement." What Filmation decided to do instead was produce 65 half hours of an animated version of their own previously produced *Ghostbusters*... with a different spin from the other version.

This version featured the teenage sons of the live-action busters Jake Kong and Eddie Spencer who (along with their father's gorilla assistant Tracy, and a gaggle of ghostbusting gimmicks, one of which was the flying, talking "Ghost Buggy") set out in pursuit of the sinister spectre Prime Evil and his squad of fellow spooks. The busters could also always count on the assistance of TV news reporter Jessica and their bewitching ally from the future, Futura, whom they had an encounter with on a time-travelling jaunt. In addition to everything else, the Ghost Buggy (affectionately known as "G.B.") could travel through time.

Unlike their previous efforts (*He-Man* and *She-Ra*), *Ghostbusters* was produced without a toy company partner to shoulder the production costs. Instead, Tribune Broadcasting, a major syndication player and TV station owner, shared production expenses (and a co-copyright) on the series which was very successful in its opening season... although this was at least partially due to its name more than the show itself. Scheimer and Filmation had not reckoned that Columbia themselves would get into the burgeoning syndication animation game which they did a year later with their *Real Ghostbusters* animated series. They included "The Real" to stress its movie-based origins, which were what the viewers were truly expecting when they first expected a *Ghostbuster's* cartoon. The Columbia/DIC-produced

version sustained a hugely successful syndication and ABC Saturday morning run, while Filmation's "original" *Ghostbusters* faded from view after a couple of seasons in syndication...ironically like the ghosts they "busted."

GHOSTBUSTERS
- [ ] THE HEADLESS HORSEMAN CAPER
- [ ] THE RANSOM OF EDDIE SPENCER
- [ ] LIKE FATHER, LIKE SON
- [ ] GHOSTNAPPERS
- [ ] CURSE OF THE DIAMOND OF GLOOM
- [ ] THAT'S NO ALIEN
- [ ] TRAIN TO DOOM-DE-DOOM-DOOM
- [ ] THE GREAT GHOST GORILLA
- [ ] A FREIND IN NEED
- [ ] THE WAY YOU ARE
- [ ] BANISH THAT BANSHEE
- [ ] COUNTRY COUSIN
- [ ] KNIGHT OF TERROR
- [ ] A COLD WINTER NIGHT
- [ ] LITTLE BIG BAT
- [ ] THE FOURTH GHOSTBUSTER
- [ ] PHANTOM OF THE BIG APPLE
- [ ] THE WHITE WHALE
- [ ] SHADES OF DRACULA
- [ ] FATHER KNOWS BEST
- [ ] SCARE PLANE
- [ ] BACK TO THE PAST
- [ ] GOING APE
- [ ] DOGGONE WEREWOLF
- [ ] BEFFLY LEADS THE WAY
- [ ] WITCH'S STEW
- [ ] GHOSTBUNGLERS
- [ ] THE BAD OLD DAYS
- [ ] THE PRINCEESS AND THE TROLL
- [ ] THE SLEEPING DRAGON
- [ ] WHITHER WHY
- [ ] PRETEND FRIENDS
- [ ] OUTLAW IN-LAWS
- [ ] CYMAN'S REVENGE
- [ ] SECOND CHANCE
- [ ] NO 'MO SNOW
- [ ] MUMMY DEAREST
- [ ] THE BATTLE FOR GHOST COMMAND
- [ ] TRACY COME BACK
- [ ] LASER AND FUTURE ROCK
- [ ] INSIDE OUT
- [ ] THE BIND THAT TIES
- [ ] PRIME EVIL'S GOOD DEED
- [ ] HE WENT BRATAWAY
- [ ] THE HAUNTING OF GIZMO
- [ ] WACY WAX MUSEUM
- [ ] EDDIE TAKES CHARGE
- [ ] THE LOOKING-GLASS WARRIOR
- [ ] MAZE CAVES
- [ ] RUNAWAY CHOO-CHOO

THE NEW ADVENTURES OF GILLIGAN

Broadcast History:
Network Premiere: ABC, September, 1974 Saturday Mornings
ABC, September, 1976 Sunday Mornings

Syndicated Premiere:
GROOVIE GOOLIES AND FRIENDS Fall, 1987

Producers: Norm Prescott, Lou Scheimer
Creative Director: Don Christensen
Executive Consultant: Sherwood Schwartz
Writers: Marc Richards, Bob Ogle, Jim Ryan, Bill Danch, Chuck Menville, Len Jansen

Principal Characters and Voices:
GILLIGAN (Willy Gilligan)..............................Bob Denver
THE SKIPPER (Janas Grumby)..........................Alan Hale, Jr.
THURSTON HOWELL III................................. Jim Bakus
MRS. LOVEY HOWELL III..........................Natalie Schafer
GINGER GRANT / MARY ANN SUMMERS........................
...
..............................Jane Webb (billed as "Jane Edwards")
THE PROFESSOR (Roy Hinkley)....................Russell Johnson
SNUBBY (Pet Monkey)............................... Lou Scheimer

After ABC's rating success with *The Brady Kids* animated series (based on Sherwood Schwartz' hit live-action *The Brady Bunch* series), the network sought to capture lightning in the bottle a second time. They noticed the proliferation of animated versions of popular sitcoms and were eager to pounce upon Schwartz and Filmation's pitch of an animated series based on Schwartz's '60's sitcom hit, *Gilligan's Island*

animation by FILMATION ☐

(which was in syndicated reruns and was registering huge demographic ratings among kids and teens).

Using scripts based upon the first season's *Gilligan's Island* episodes, *The New Adventures of Gilligan* used a new theme (written by Schwartz, who also wrote the original theme, but this time it was sung by the original cast) to retell the tale of the crew and passengers of the S.S. Minnow…a boat whose three-hour tour turned into a fifteen-year stay on an uncharted isle in the South Pacific. In addition, seeking to emulate the acclaim and adulation given to CBS's *Fat Albert and the Cosby Kids* series for it's educational morals within their animated antics, members of the same advisory team located at UCLA also supervised the Gilligan animated scripts… thus stressing the castaways' learning experiences in living with each other. These incidents occurred both in the main stories and in the minute-long tag at the end of each episode. A word about minute-long tags (which incidentally do not appear in the show's syndicated reruns): up to 1973, each of the three networks (CBS, NBC, ABC) used varying lengths of show content vs. commercial content in their Saturday morning programming half hours. Before, network and syndicated half hours were basically 22 minutes of actual show content and eight minutes of commercials. In addition, the three networks typically ordered 16 half hour episodes per season. But in 1973, NBC cut its series' orders to 13.5 hours per season and added two extra minutes of story content into each episode produced. The next season, when the reduction in children's network commercial time became mandatory, the other two networks inserted extra material in their series… although it was left to the studios to determine how to utilize the material. Hanna-Barbera, for instance, inserted extra story segments into its 74-75 series. Filmation opted to add either minute-long educational tags (*Gilligan's Island*), lengthened song sequences (*Fat Albert and the Cosby Kids*), or scenes from upcoming episodes (*U.S. of Archie*). These sequences were later more easily dropped from the shows once they entered syndication where increased commercial content necessitated their removal.

Back to the show itself: the majority of the *Gilligan's Island*

cast, typecast by the original series and not doing too much other work, returned to provide the voices for their animated counterparts, except for Dawn Wells (Mary Ann) who at the time was doing theater, and Tina Louise (Ginger), who felt she was so typecast as a dim redhead that she not only refused to come back to the cartoon but even refused to let Filmation use her likeness, which is why the animated Ginger was a platinum blonde. Filmation's main female voice artist at the time, Jane Webb, performed both Mary Ann and Ginger's roles. To give the illusion that two actresses were used for the cartoon's title tune refrain and voice placing ("...the movie star, the Professor, and Mary Ann..."), Jane used her maiden name. Hence, "Jane Edwards" for the "Mary Ann" credit, and her married and professional "Jane Webb" for the "Ginger" credit. *The New Adventures of Gilligan* was the #1 Saturday morning series in it's maiden season.

THE NEW ADVENTURES OF GILLIGAN (1974)
- [ ] OFF LIMITS
- [ ] LOONEY MOON
- [ ] RAVEN MAD
- [ ] FATHER OF HIS ISLAND
- [ ] WRONG WAY ROBOT (YEAH, WOULD YOU WANT YOUR SISTER TO MARRY ONE?)
- [ ] OPENING NIGHT
- [ ] LOLLIPOP CASSEROLE
- [ ] THE LONERS (NOBODY'S ISLAND)
- [ ] THE GO TRIP (KON-TACKY)
- [ ] THE OLYMPIAD
- [ ] IN THEIR OWN IMAGE
- [ ] THE DISAPPEARING ACT
- [ ] A SINKING FEELING
- [ ] THE RELUCTANT HERO
- [ ] THE SAME OLD DREAM
- [ ] SPUTTERING

(1975)
- [ ] SUPER GILLIAN
- [ ] MARONNED AGAIN
- [ ] LIVE AND LET LIVE
- [ ] WHEELS ON PARADE
- [ ] THE MOVIE MAKER
- [ ] SILENCE IS LEADEN
- [ ] THE GREAT TRAIN ROBBERY

GILLIGAN'S PLANET

Broadcast History:
Network History: CBS Saturday Mornings, 1982-83

Executive Producers: Norm Prescott / Lou Scheimer
Producer: Don Christensen
Creative Consultant: Sherwood Schwartz
Writers: Marc Richards, Paul Dini, Tom Ruegger, Robby London
Characters and Voices: SAME as
THE NEW ADVENTURES OF GILLIGAN
EXCEPT:
MARY ANN / GINGER .... Dawn Wells

CBS, noting the animated Gilligan's success in syndication, decided to ignore the fact that three years before, the *Gilligan's Island* cast had finally been rescued from their island, and, to boost their sagging Saturday morning ratings, commissioned a new Gilligan animated series. This time, they took the incongruous premise to new heights.

The castaways manage to convert the wreckage of the Minnow into a rocketship which they use to leave the island…only to end up being stranded on a mysterious planet (not a new situation for Bob "Gilligan" Denver as, several seasons earlier, he played an astronaut stranded on a distant planet in CBS' live-action Saturday morning series *Far-Out Space Nuts*, which was produced by Sid and Marty Krofft in 1975). With the exception of a new alien pet to replace "Snubby" (also reminiscent of *Space Nuts'* "Honk"), the cast remained the same with the addition of the return of Dawn Wells, who not only played Mary Ann's voice but mimicked the premise of a live-action Gilligan's Island episode by portraying Ginger's voice as well.

GILLIGAN'S PLANET
☐ I DREAM OF GENIE
☐ TURNABOUT IS FAIR PLAY
☐ LET SLEEPING MINNOWS LIE
☐ JOURNEY TO THE CENTER OF
☐ GILLIGAN'S PLANET
☐ AMAZING COLOSSAL GILLIGAN
☐ BUMPER TO BUMPER
☐ ROAD TO BOOM
☐ TOO MANY GILLIGANS
☐ SPACE PIRATES
☐ INVADERS OF THE LOST BARQUE
☐ WINGS
☐ SUPER GILLIGAN
☐ GILLIGAN'S ARMY

THE GROOVIE GOOLIES

Broadcast History:
SABRINA AND THE GROOVIE GOOLIES
Network Premiere: CBS, September, 1970, Saturday Mornings

Syndicated History:
THE GROOVIE GOOLIES AND FRIENDS
Syndication Premiere: Fall, 1987

Executive Producers: Louis Scheimer, Norman Prescott
Producer: Hal Sutherland

Principal Characters:
COUNT DRACULA "DRAC" / BATSO…………Larry Storch

HAGATHA / AUNT HILDA / AUNT ZELDA / HAGATHA / BELLA LA GHOSTLY / BROOM-HILDA / SABRINA…………
………………………………………………………………Jane Webb
FRANKIE / WOLFIE / MUMMY / GHOULA-HAND…………
…………………………………………………………Howard Morris
BONAPART / DR. JEKYLL-HYDE / BATSO / HAUNTLEROY …………………………………… Larry Mann

The Groovie Goolies, an eclectic collection of merry monsters, joked, sang and frolicked in eerie Horrible Hall. The owner was none other than that master sorcerer, Count Dracula, known as "Drac," who napped in a comfy casket and flapped about as a transformed vampire bat. It was convenient at times, particularly when he was being pursued by the Lovesick Loveseat, an amorous sofa that continually tried to embrace him. Hagatha, Dracula's plump wife, gave lessons in low cuisine on "From the Witch's Kitchen." Most of the time she slaved over a hot cauldron, aided by Broom Hilda, her mischievous bristly broom. In her spare time, the three-hundred-year-old crone listened to her advisor, the Magic Mirror, and gossiped on the Tel-a-Bone with her sister, Nagatha.

A large lovable lug, Frankie (Frankenstein's monster), was fond of dimwitted pranks and bizarre bedtime stories. Rover was his affectionate pet dinosaur and Orville, The Thing-Eating Plant, his pet gluttonous gardenia, was a voracious consumer of anything animal, vegetable, or mineral. Providing advice for the lovelorn and the daily Horror-scope via the Tel-Bone, Bella La Ghostly was Horrible Hall's morbidly glamorous switchboard operator. Hip and hairy, Wolfie (Wolfman) was the athletic type. Always on the move, he whizzed about via surfboard, skateboard, and his custom-built "Wolfwagon." His pet was Fido, a

flying piranha fish. An accident-prone skeleton, Bonapart literally fell into pieces in a heap of disconnected bones whenever he was involved in a collision. Bonapart's buddy, the Mummy, was a TV news announcer and a first-aid expert who became unwound a bit too easily.

Among the other macabre characters, Dr. Jekyll-Hyde was a schizophrenic two-headed doctor who made haunted house calls; Ratso and Batso, pint-sized meanies modeled on Eddie Wolfgang Munster, son of *The Munsters* (CBS, 1964-1966), who constantly brewed up trouble in their "Inventory" lab; Hauntleroy, a spirited, practical joker, who was a coward at heart; Ghoulihand, seemingly all thumbs, was a giant hand like "The Thing" on *The Addams Family* that served as Drak's handyman and occasionally played the piano; Tiny Tomb and Miss Icky, a long-haired ukulele player and his girlfriend; and Askit Casket, a lid-flapping source of wit and wisdom.

The only normal-looking visitor to the cobwebbed castle was the winsome *Sabrina, The Teenage Witch*, who nevertheless managed to connive and cavort with the worst of them. Originally packaged as the hour-long series *Sabrina and The Groovie Goolies*, under the fatherly eye of Fred Silverman, head of CBS daytime programming, the ghoulish group was created to support the young sorceress when Sabrina was separated in 1970 from *The Archies*. One of the most humorous animated comedies produced by Filmation, although overly cluttered with characters and "things," its variety-comedy-music format was borrowed largely from the prime time ratings hit, *Rowan and Martin's Laugh-In* (NBC, 1968-1973). A "Weird Windows" segment featured two-liner gags. Hagatha told her bedtime stories with off-beat casting. The bandaged banterer reported the ghoulish news in the Mummy Wrap-Up, and Frankie appeared in sketches as Sooper Gool, "able to leap haunted houses in a single bound." Also musically inclined, The Groovie Goolies gathered for a rock tune in each show, in such originals as "C'mon, C'mon to the Goolie Picnic" and "The Goolie Garden," where the strangest things vegetate.

The series completed its CBS run on September, 1972, and returned October, 1975, on ABC, replacing the first half hour of the network's failed *Uncle Croc's Block*.

GROOVIE GHOULIES

- [ ] 1-2-3-
- [ ] CLING CLANG
- [ ] WHAT'S IN THE BAG
- [ ] GOOLIE PICNIC
- [ ] GOOLIE GARDEN
- [ ] FEED THE GHOST SOME GARLIC
- [ ] FRANKIE
- [ ] NOISES
- [ ] MONSTER TRIO
- [ ] GOOLIE SWING
- [ ] WITCHES BREW
- [ ] GOOL SCHOOL
- [ ] SHADOWS
- [ ] SAVE YOUR GOOD LOVIN'
- [ ] DARLIN' DARLIN'
- [ ] AT THE FIRST ANNUAL SEMI FORMAL
- [ ] COMBINATION MEET THE MONSTER POPULATION PARTY
- [ ] LIGHTS OUT
- [ ] WHEN THE MOON IS FULL
- [ ] WHEN I GROW UP
- [ ] WHERE YOU GOING LITTLE GHOUL
- [ ] MONSTERS ON PARADE
- [ ] MIDNIGHT
- [ ] BE KIND TO MONSTER WEEK
- [ ] LITTLE TEXAS GOOLIE
- [ ] SUPER GHOUL

THE HARDY BOYS

Broadcast History:
Network Premiere: ABC, September, 1969 Saturday Morning

Syndicated History:
Distributor: 20th Century-Fox Television

Producers: Louis Scheimer, Norman Prescott
Director: Hal Sutherland
Writers: Ken Sobol, H.F. Mauberly, Eric Blair, David Melmoth

Principal Characters and Voices:
FRANK HARDY / CHUBBY MORTON...Dallas McKennon
JOE HARDY / PETE JONES / FENTON HARDY......................
....Byron Kane
WANDA KAY BRECKENRIDGE /GERTUDE HARDY..........
....Jane Webb

Juvenile novelist Franklin W. Dixon's (real name, Edward L. Stratemeyer) teenage detectives, Frank and Joe Hardy, became the stars of Saturday morning's first animated mystery-adventure series when *The Hardy Boys* premiered in 1969. Aside from that, the show was a groundbreaker for several other reasons. It was the first Saturday morning cartoon to feature a black character, Pete Jones, and it was the first cartoon to address the real-world element of "cocaine smuggling" in an animated kid's context. Perhaps most important, it was the first cartoon to include 30-second PSA's (Public Service Announcements) at the end of each program in which the animated Hardys addressed the audience on-camera about the perils of smoking, drinking, drugs, and positive advice on seat belt use.

With the series created after Robert Kennedy's assassination, which spurred an outcry against "violent" cartoons on television, the format problems that could have occurred because of the stories' bent toward physical confrontations between the good and bad guys were avoided by staging all the physical battles off-camera, thus forcing the viewers to use their imaginations as to the seriousness of the fight scenes.

Also adding to the different format of The Hardy Boys series, and inspired by rival CBS's success with Filmation's Archies singing group the previous season, was The Hardy Boys singing group, which sang a pop musical number in the middle of each half hour in animated form. A live-action version of the group performed the opening and closing titles as well as recording two albums and actually hitting the American Bandstand pop charts with "Wheels" and "Love Train."

Another subtle change was introduced into Filmation's cartoons with this series. In fact, it was so subtle that you would have to hang around until the end of the credits to notice it. Filmation producers Norm Prescott and Lou Scheimer alternated their presidency of the company from year-to-year, with each serving as president on alternate years; Lou's name was on top of Norm's one season, and Norm's was on top the next in the producer credits. They arrived at the point to give their names "equal placement" in the producer's credit. They put their names in an animating circle, around the producer's/executive produc-

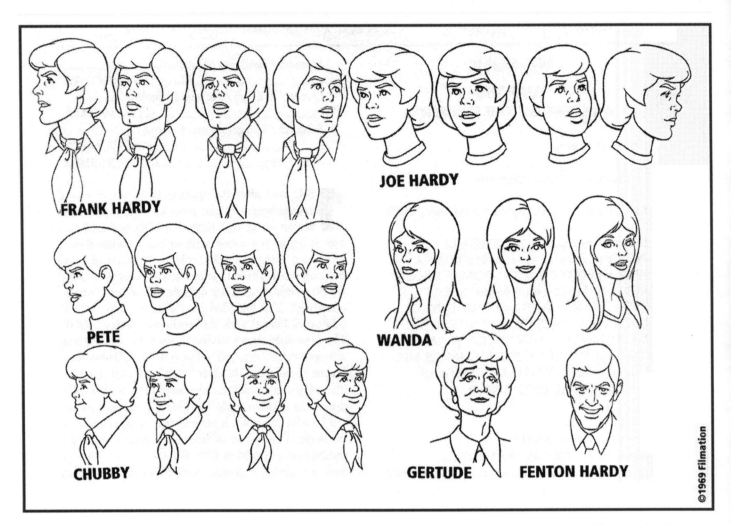

er's credit, with the name that started animating around signifying the company president that season, while making both look "equal" in the end credits.

(**Author's Note:** *As a youngster, I vividly remember Pete's admonishment against smoking, it being the first time a black cartoon character spoke to me about the perils of smoking. So I credit the show for my not smoking now.*

One image that really impressed me, and I've carried in my mind since, was that of the ABC Saturday Morning Preview Special that year hosted by the cast of the live-action ABC

The real-life band members whose pictures were used on the album and comic book covers were Deven English (Wanda Kay), Norbet 'Nibs' Soltysiak (Chubby Morton), Reed Kailing (Frank Hardy), Jeff Taylor (Joe Hardy) and Bob Crowder (Pete Jones) who was once a drummer for Jerry Butler, Fontella Bass, Shirelles & Esquires.

sitcom The Ghost and Mrs. Muir. *In that, they ran a preview sequence of the animated Hardy Boys, which the cast watched on their TV. Later, when Mrs. Muir's kids clapped their approval, the ghostly captain, played by Edward Mulhare, used his "magical" powers to create a surprise for the kids and the audience as he "materiaized" the live-action Hardy Boys to perform in the Muir's living room...a very impressive image for a cartoon-loving youth.)*

THE HARDY BOYS
- ☐ THE SECRET WARNING
- ☐ THE VIKING SYMBOL MYSTERY
- ☐ THE SECRET OF THE CAVES
- ☐ THE SECRET OF THE OLD MILL
- ☐ THE MISSING CHUMS
- ☐ THE MYSTERY OF THE DESERT GIANTS
- ☐ THE MYSTERY CABIN ISLAND
- ☐ HUNTING FOR HIDDEN GOLD
- ☐ THE MYSTERY OF THE AZTEC WARRIOR
- ☐ THE HIDDEN HARBOR MYSTERY
- ☐ GHOST AT SKELETON ROCK
- ☐ MYSTERY OF CHINESE JUNK
- ☐ THE SHORE ROAD MYSTERY
- ☐ WHAT HAPPENED AT MIDNIGHT
- ☐ THE SIGN OF THE CROOKED ARROW
- ☐ THE CLUE IN THE EMBERS
- ☐ THE CLUE THE SCREECHING OWL
- ☐ THE HOUSE ON THE CLIFF
- ☐ MYSTERY OF THE SPIRAL BRIDGE
- ☐ THE YELLOW FEATHER MYSTERY
- ☐ THE MYSTERY OF DEVILS PAW
- ☐ THE SINISTER SIGN POST
- ☐ THE MELTED COINS

HE-MAN AND THE MASTERS OF THE UNIVERSE

Broadcast History:
Syndication Premiere - September, 1983

Cable Premiere: USA Network, September, 1989

Executive Producer: Lou Scheimer

Production Director: Hal Sutherland
Writers: Robby London, Tom Ruegger, Ron & Sam Schultz, Marc Scott Zicree, Larry Ditillio, Paul Dini, J. Michael Reaves, Byrnne Stephens, Anis Diamond, David Wise, Susan "Misty" Stewart, Marc Richards, Mel Gilden, Jeffery O'hare, Douglas Booth, Arthur Browne Jr.

Principal Characters and Voices:
PRINCE ADAM / HE-MAN / RAM MAN .... John Erwin
MERMAN / BEASTMAN / SKELETOR .... Alan Oppenheimer
QUEEN / EVIL-LYN / SORCERESS / TEELA .... Linda Gary
BATTLECAT / GRINGER / MAN-AT-ARMS .... Eric Gunden
ORKO / KING .... Lou Scheimer

1982 was, after the spectacular production and ratings heights of the previous season, the worst season up to that time that Filmation had ever had. It began as a season with so much production to be created that the studio broke its tradition of never sending work abroad (starting a production trend which would eventually cripple Filmation's way of operating). This included producing a series in 1982 (*Gilligan's Planet*) with the smallest staff since 1966's The *New Adventures of Superman* series (and ratings so low that CBS first had to fast-order *The Dukes* from Hanna-Barbera to save their Saturday

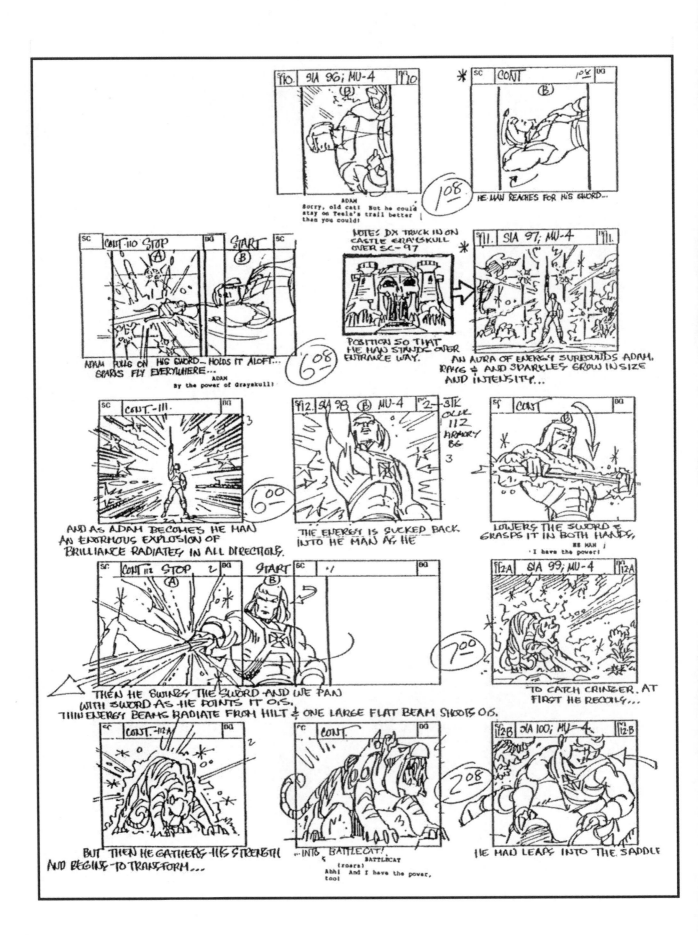

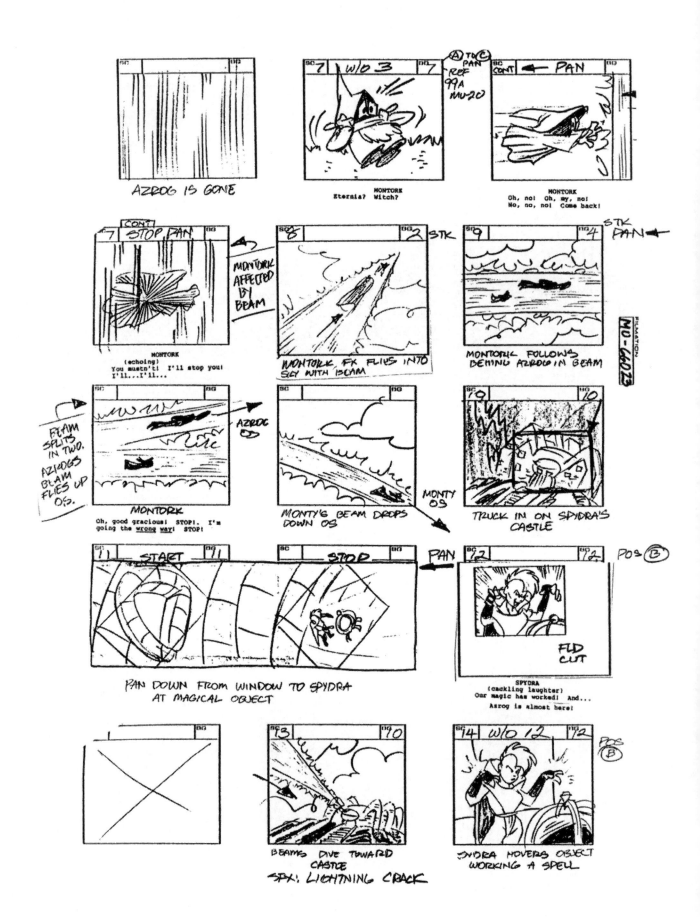

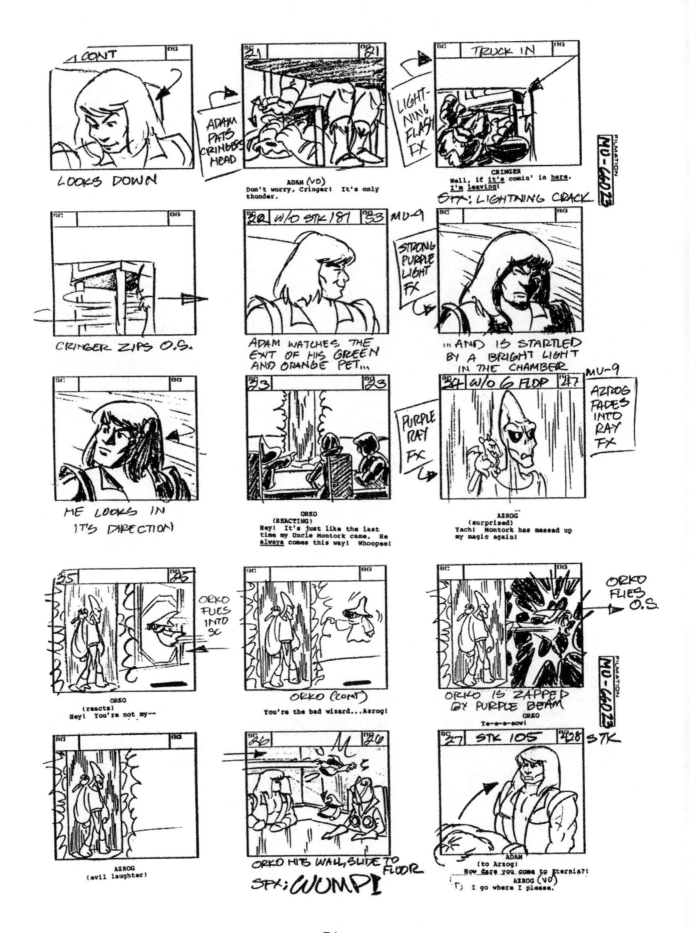

morning schedule and vowed to never order another series from Filmation... a decision made by NBC the previous season and by ABC in 1976). It seemed that Filmation was on the verge of going out of business. It took a series Filmation had produced in 1981 that failed, an innovative new marketing strategy, and government policy changes to not only bring the company back from the dead but create what would eventually become the biggest boom to hit the animation industry since the production of animation for Saturday mornings back in the '60's.

Back in the 1960's, a syndicated animated series called *Linus the Lionhearted* was produced, centering around the comical misadventures of a variety of characters who originally served as "spokesmen" for the line of Post cereals, with the Post company serving as the series' co-producer and major sponsor. Due to some consumer complaints, which were exacerbated a few years later when the Mattel toy company produced an animated series for ABC based on their *Hot Wheels* toy line, the government regulatory agency, the Federal Communications Commission (FCC) eventually ruled that children's animated series could not feature characters appearing in stories on the show that could also be featured in ads advertising the products the characters were featured in, on the basis that those were, in essence, "half-hour commercials."

Twenty years later the young Reagan Administration, believing in less governmental interference on the broadcast sector, caused the FCC to modify their policy. Among those changes were the modification of the "half-hour commercials" policy to one that did not forbid the production of animated series featuring toy or cereal characters in commercials featuring products as long as those commercials were not broadcast in the body of the half-hour itself. With that out of the way, all that was needed was someone with the money to finance such a venture and the guts to circumvent standard television operating procedure since the networks were, at the time, still skittish about the concept.

Enter Mattel Toys, among other things, the creators of the most popular girls' toys in the world—the Barbie doll. Deciding in 1982 that dolls' marketed to boys could prove to become a lucrative product, they developed the concept of smaller (five-inch) dolls to be called "action figures," that emphasized the world of fantasy and action adventure in their play. Impressed by Filmation's 1981 series *Blackstar*, they contracted the studio to animate a series of 30-second commercial spots for their newly-developed toy concept now called *He-Man and the Masters of the Universe*.

He-Man, while sounding rather basic and simplistic, was the strongest tested name among the kids' focus groups, and the Masters of the Universe actually related mainly to He-Man's adversaries. After enthusiastic test results, (somewhat ironically) the 30-second spots were shelved because of an idea encouraged by the government's deregulation...instead of just doing 30-second or one-minute commercials, it was decided to use a portion of Mattel's 100 million dollar advertising budget to produce an daily animated series highlighting the adventures of the characters featured in the toy line.

Since by this time the networks had set their series orders at 13 weeks (thus ensuring that each episode would run four times during a 52-week season), and since Mattel wanted to maximize exposure of the concept, it was decided to create a series of 65 episodes (with the same new episode/re-run ratio of the weekend programming).

Another important reason for Mattel's alliance with Filmation, in addition to the aforementioned others, was their

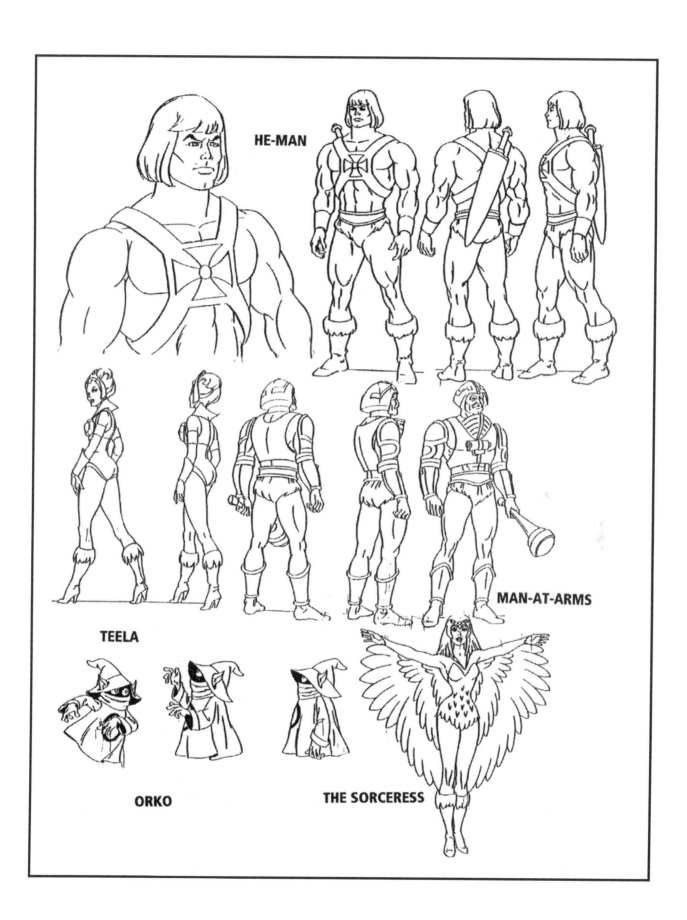

ownership by Group W/ Westinghouse, one of the then-leading forces in broadcast syndication, which in turn was vital to their plans to sidestep the reluctant networks (Mattel not forgetting their experience with ABC and Hot Wheels). The 30-second spots, which boasted more surface detail and fuller animation due to their bigger budget, thus became the promotional film the syndicator took to the NATPE (National Association of Television Programming Executives) Convention to convince station owners to go with the heretofore-unknown and financially risky idea: all new animation for kids in the daily afternoon time-period. The rest, as they say, is history.

Premiering that fall (1983) to tremendous ratings and demographics (and accompanying toy sales), the adventures of He-Man and his friends on the land of Eternia vs. the machinations of the villainous Skeletor and his mob of malefactor mutants (along with competing studio DIC's *Inspector Gadget*) forever changed the face of animation by, among other things, 1) Bringing a whole new audience (and profits) to an arena previously dominated by sit-com reruns and game/talk shows; 2) bringing an influx of thousands of new animators and many new studios into the animation mix; 3) reducing the dominance of networks in the involvement of kids programming and, last but not least, 4) increasing the scope of licensors/toy company television production in ways that, at the time, could barely be imagined. The *He-Man* series lasted 130 episodes produced over a three-year period and an hour-length Christmas special, not to mention launching its own successful spin-off, *She-Ra,, Princess of Power* and feature film, *He-Man and the Masters of the Universe*, featuring Dolph Lungren as He Man and Frank Langella as Skeletor.

HE-MAN AND THE MASTERS OF THE UNIVERSE
- ☐ THE COSMIC COMET
- ☐ THE SHAPING STAFF
- ☐ DISAPPEARING ACT
- ☐ DIAMOND RAY OF DISAPPEARANCE
- ☐ SHE DEMON OF PHANTOS
- ☐ TEELA'S QUEST
- ☐ THE CURSE OF THE SPELLSTONE
- ☐ THE TIME CORRIDOR
- ☐ THE DRAGON INVASION
- ☐ A FRIEND IN NEED
- ☐ MASKS OF POWER
- ☐ EVIL-LYN'S EVIL PLOT
- ☐ LIKE FATHER, LIKE DAUGHER
- ☐ COLOSSOR AWAKES
- ☐ A BEASTLY SIDESHOW
- ☐ REGIN OF THE MONSTERS
- ☐ DAIMAR THE DEMON
- ☐ CREATURES FROM THE TAR SWAMP
- ☐ QUEST FOR HE-MAN
- ☐ DAWN OF DRAGOON
- ☐ THE ROYAL COUSIN
- ☐ SONG OF CELICE
- ☐ THE RETURN OF ORKO'S UNCLE
- ☐ WIZARD OF STONE MOUNTAIN
- ☐ EVILSEED
- ☐ ORDEAL IN THE DARKLANDS
- ☐ ORKO'S FAVORITE UNCLE

- TEMPLE OF THE SUN
- CITY BENEATH THE SEA
- TEELA'S TRAIL
- DREE ELLE'S RETURN
- GAME PLAN
- EYE OF THE BEHOLDER
- QUEST FOR THE SWORD
- CASTLE OF HEROES
- THE ONCE AND FUTURE DUKE
- THE WITCH AND THE WARRIOR
- THE RETURN OF GRANAMYR
- PAWNS OF THE GAME MASTER
- GOLDEN DISKS OF KNOWLEDGE
- THE HUNTSMAN
- THE REMEDY
- THE HEART OF A GIANT

- THE DEFECTION
- PRINCE ADAM NO MORE
- THE TAKING OF GRAYSKULL
- A TALE OF TWO CITIES
- SEARCH FOR THE VHO
- THE STARCHILD
- THE DRAGON'S GIFT
- THE SLEEPERS AWAKEN
- THE SEARCH
- IT'S NOT MY FAULT
- VALLEY OF POWER
- TROUBLE IN ARCADIA
- HOUSE OF SHOKOTI (Parts I and II)
- DOUBLE EDGED SWORD
- THE MYSTERY OF MAN-E-FACES
- THE REGION OF ICE
- ORKO'S MISSING MAGIC
- ETERNAL DARKNESS
- KEEPER OF THE ANCIENT RUINS
- RETURN OF EVIL
- RETURN OF GRYPHON

JOURNEY TO THE CENTER OF THE EARTH

Broadcast History:
Premiere: ABC, September, 1967, Saturday Morning

Executive Producers: Louis Scheimer, Norman Prescott
Director: Hal Sutherland
Story Editor: Ken Sobol

Principal Characters and Voices:
PROFESSOR OLIVER LINDENBROOK / COUNT SACCNUS SON…..........................……Ted Knight
CINDY LINDENBROOK…………..................…....Jane Webb
ALEC McEWEN / LARS / TORG /GERTRUDE (Lar's pet duck)….. Pat Harrington

With the overwhelming success of Filmation's first animated Saturday morning series, 1966's *The New Adventures of Superman*, whose average 55 share tied it with Hanna-Barbera's *Space Ghost* and Filmation's 1968 *The Archie Show* as the top-rated Saturday morning series of all time, the fledging studio was finally on the map. It was also on a creative course that would serve well over the next decade: basing its creative development for the most part on already established concepts, rather than developing its own original series. This also gave Filmation's programs an instant name-value recognition that offset main rival Hanna-

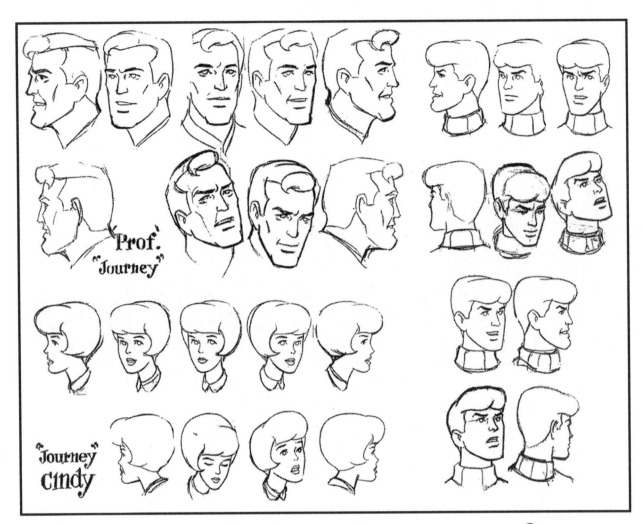

Barbera's proven, creative track record, which it brought to projects. Filmation decided to not just go after already established "kids'" properties but various "adult-oriented" properties that could be adopted into children's programs. One concept that interested ABC, just entering into the Saturday morning kids' market after rival CBS's resounding successes the season before, was a series based on the 1959 20th Century Fox sci-fi adventure movie Journey to the Center of the Earth, itself based on Jules Verne's 1865 French science fiction classic.

The Filmation series followed the adventures of a small group of explorers seeking the secrets that lay in the Earth's core. Using this as a starting point, they began with the discovery of the long-lost trail of explorer Arnie Saccnuson, who had managed to find Professor Oliver Lindenbrook's hidden subterranean passage that led through a mysterious labyrinth of caverns to the center of the Earth. Accompanied by his young niece, Cindy, her classmate, Alec McEwen, their guide, Lars, and his pet duck, Gertrude. For purely scientific purposes, Lindenbrook uses the cryptic clues left behind by Arnie to discover the secrets of the center of the Earth, which he intend to use for mankind's benefit.

However, Arnie's last living descendant, the evil Count Saccnusson, decided, for purely altruistic purposes, to seek the secrets of his ancestor's discovery for himself. Using those secrets to promote his own power-mad agenda of world conquest, Saccnusson ordered his monstrous man-servant, Torg, to set off an explosive charge to destroy the Lindenbrook expedition. The charge instead obliterates the only entrance to the trail, effectively trapping both parties under the Earth's surface and forcing both

groups into a death-defying race to reach the center of the Earth. He wanted not just to discover what Arnie had found, but to find the secret of the way back to the Earth's surface. On the way, the parties battled not only each other, but also tribes of lost civilizations, prehistoric creatures, and unnatural phenomena as they wend their perilous way on their quest.

This series was responsible for two particular impacts on the Saturday morning landscape. It was the first series to establish one of Saturday morning's enduring genres: the "quest" series, a serialized or at least continuing format involving a group of characters and their search for a particular "McGuffin," or object upon which the series would basically conclude upon discovery or acquisition of said object. In this case, Journey to the Center of the Earth would officially end once the Lindenbrooks and/or Count Saccnusson reached the center. Most "quest" series, and this series was no exception, seldom "ended" because ending the show would usually be saved for a planned second season pick-up of new episodes...and the vast majority of these series never received a second season renewal.

(Author's Note: The other impact was Filmation's intro- duction of Ted Knight, its answer to Mel Blanc, to the ranks of adventure vocals. Knight later starred as "Ted Baxter" in the Mary Tyler Moore Show, *followed by his own series,* Too Close For Comfort, *and* The Ted Knight Show, *before dying of cancer. The ubiquitous Mr. Knight portrayed not only the leads but also almost all the supporting players in the majority of series he vocalized for Filmation. Also of note here is the other male voice for* Journey to the Center of the Earth, *Pat Harrington Jr., who later found sitcom fame as the character "Schneider" in the long-running* One Day at a Time *series.)*

JOURNEY TO THE CENTER OF THE EARTH
☐ THE LABYRINTH BUILDERS
☐ LAND OF THE DEAD
☐ THE CREATURE WORLD
☐ REVENGE OF THE FOSSILS
☐ THE DOOMED ISLAND
☐ RETURN OF GULLIVER
☐ TRAIL OF GOLD
☐ OCEAN OF DESTRUCTION
☐ THE FROZEN FURIES
☐ ARENA OF FEAR
☐ CAVEMAN CAPTIVES
☐ OCEAN OF DESTRUCTION
☐ PERILS OF VOLCANO
☐ LIVING CITY
☐ CREATURE SWAMP
☐ THE CAVE MEN
☐ SLEEPING SLAVES
☐ MOTH'S DOOM

KID SUPER POWER HOUR with SHAZAM!

Live-action producer: ARTHUR NADEL
Writer/Story Editor: COSLOUGH JOHNSON

Hero High Principal Characters and Actors/Voices:
CAPTAIN CALIFORNIA............................Christopher Hilber
MISTY MAGIC...Geri Feilds
GLORIOUS GAL...Becky Perle
DIRTY TRIXIE...Maylo McCashin
WEATHERMAN..Ken Sansom
PRINCIPAL SAMPSON ....
.... ALAN OPPENHEIMER
MISS GRIMM.. ERICA SCHEIMER

SHAZAM! Principle Characters and Voices:
CAPTIAN MARVEL / BILLY BATSON ....Burr Middleton
FREDDY FREEDMAN / CAPTAIN MARVEL,JR...................
.... Barry Gordon
MARY BATSON / MARY MARVEL .... Dawn Jeffory
UNCLE DUDLEY / UNCLE MARVEL ....
....Alan Oppenheimer
STERLING MORRIS ....Lou Scheimer
NARRATOR .... Norm Prescott
DR. THADDEUS BODOG SIVANA / TAWKY TAWNY......
.... Alan Oppenheimer

Originally pitched to NBC as an animated version of the Super Archie's concept featured in Archie Comics (and trading in with Filmation's long-standing relationship with the Archie characters), NBC Head of Programming, Fred Silverman (remembering the failure of *The New Archie/Sabrina Hour* several seasons before-1977-78) was receptive to the idea of cloaking the Archie personalities into an all-new group of characters. Filmation, finally getting the chance to own a potentially hot franchise for a change, recre-

ated Riverdale High as "SuperHero High" (later shortened to Hero High as DC and Marvel Comics co-owned the trademarked word "superhero"). They then created new characters with "Archie-esque" parallels: Captain California (Archie), Glorious Gal (Betty), Rex Ruthless (Reggie), Dirty Trixie (Veronica), and Weatherman (Jughead). These five joined music-loving Punk Rock and studious black teen Misty Magic (the daughter of the town's police chief) at Hero High...a school for up-and-coming heroes run by ex-superhero/school principal Sampson (Mr. Weatherbee with a much better looking body) and Miss Grimm (Miss Grundy). Their on and off campus exploits were featured in 12 and eight-minute stories. These were integrated with an 18-minute *Shazam!*, starring Captain Marvel, with each new show. The Captain Marvel character was previously produced by Filmation as a very successful live-action Saturday series on CBS for four seasons (1974-78). Shazam! was produced while on Fred Silverman's watch at CBS and satisfied his desire to have characters of *Hero High*, who had already been established with kid audiences. With *Hero High*, Filmation was able to do something they couldn't do with the Archie cast—the characters hosted *Kid Super* in a format similar to Archie's Funhouse (telling jokes as the heroes, singing songs in front of a live-audience), but this time they were able to perform as a live-action actor's cast for their resemblance of the animated character concepts (the kids this time were the daughters of other Filmation employees). But plans for the "heroes'" album and concert tour were cancelled when the show itself was canned the following season.

In 1981, Filmation produced an animated version of Shazam! reuniting them with the Captain Marvel character they had produced in live-action back in the '70's, marking one of the few times the same studio produced both animated and live-action versions of the same character (*Ed. Note: SHAZAM! live-action for more information on the origins of Captain Marvel and Filmation's first incarnation*). This version, like the first planned animated version, hewed closely to the established comic characters. These featured heroes (Captain Marvel, Captain Marvel Jr., Mary Marvel, Uncle Marvel, and Tawky Tawny) and villains (Dr. Sivano, Black Adam, Ibac, Mr. Mind, and Mr. Atom) plucked straight from the comic's pages. This show fit Filmation's established pattern of showing minority characters as leads when one of the Marvels, Captain Marvel Jr.'s, secret identity was handicapped (walking with a crutch) newsboy, Freddy Freeman. It also followed the comics (and made it a little more tricky for scriptwriters) in that Billy and Mary Batson said the word "Shazam!" (the name of the wizard who gave them their powers) to become Captain Marvel and Mary Marvel. Freddy transformed by saying the name of the man who saved his life ("Captain Marvel") to become Captain Marvel Jr. (meaning that he couldn't even say his own name when hawking newspapers that featured Captain Marvel in action).

Another unusual thing about the series was its format; it was broadcast with Hero High in tandem as part of the Kid Super Power Hour with Shazam! but, rather than the usual 6-7, 11-12, or 22-24 minute segment lengths and usual thirteen episode orders, the Shazam! segments ran 18 minutes in length with only 12 episodes produced. The rationale for the former was that the Shazam! episodes used in the middle of the hour were "cliffhangers" in the second half hour. For the latter, believe it or not, nobody noticed until the end of production that only twelve episodes were made...and it was too late then to produce a thirteenth one!

HERO HIGH
☐ THE ART OF THE BALLOT
☐ WHAT'S NEWS
☐ RAT FINK REX
☐ DO THE COMPUTER STOMP

- ☐ MALT SHOP MAYHEM
- ☐ BOO WHO
- ☐ COVER TWIRL
- ☐ MY JOB IS YOURS
- ☐ GIRL OF HIS DREAMS
- ☐ THE NOT-SO-GREAT OUTDOORS
- ☐ OFF HER ROCKER
- ☐ FOLLOW THE LITTER
- ☐ JOG-A-LONG
- ☐ HE SINKS SEASHIPS
- ☐ STARFIRE, WHERE ARE YOU?
- ☐ THE CAPTIVES
- ☐ HIGH-RISE HIJINX
- ☐ TRACK RACE
- ☐ A CLONE OF HIS OWN
- ☐ GAME OF CHANCE
- ☐ THE UMPIRE STRIKES BACK
- ☐ THE HUMAN FLY
- ☐ THE BLOW-AWAY BLIMP
- ☐ BIG BANG THEORY
- ☐ LAW OF THE PACK
- ☐ A FISTFUL OF KNUCKLES

SHAZAM ! (animated)
- ☐ WHO'S WHO AT THE ZOO?
- ☐ THE INCREDIBLE CITY
- ☐ BEST SELLER
- ☐ FLIGHT 601 HAS VANISHED
- ☐ BLACK ADAM'S RETURN
- ☐ A MENACING FAMILY AFFAIR
- ☐ UNCLE DUDLEY'S WEDDING DAY
- ☐ A LITTLE SOMETHING EXTRA
- ☐ THE AIRPORT CAPER!
- ☐ MR. ATOM, THE SMASHER
- ☐ THE CIRCUS PLOT
- ☐ STAR MASTER AND THE SOLAR MIRR

LASSIE'S RESCUE RANGERS

Broadcast History:
LASSIE AND THE SPRIT OF THUNDER MOUNTAIN
Network Premiere: ABC, November, 1972
ABC Saturday Superstar Movie

LASSIE'S RESCUE RANGERS
Network Premiere: ABC, Sept., 1973, Saturday Mornings
Syndicated History:
THE GROOVIE GOOLIES AND FRIENDS

Producers: Lou Scheimer, Norm Prescott
Associate Producer: Robert F. Chenault
Director: Hal Sutherland
Writers: Chuck Menville, Len Jenson

Principal Characters and Voices:
LASSIE .... Herself
BEN TURNER... Ted Knight
LAURA TURNER / SUSAN TURNER....................Jane Webb
JACKIE TURNER...Lane Scheimer
BEN TURNER, JR. ....Hal Harvey
GENE FOX ....Keith Sutherland

In 1972, ABC decided to create a Saturday Morning series that brought a number of concepts to Saturday morning television that had previously only existed on primetime. Under the working title of *Saturday Morning at the Movies*, the series that reached the airwaves as *ABC Saturday Superstar Movie* brought several new ideas to the weekend's kid lineup: it was Saturday morning's first hour-length series that was composed of hour-length stories rather than six-minute segments, and it was the first Saturday morning series that featured a different cast of characters in each episode...thus making it the first Saturday morning kids' anthology (as well as serving as a pilot "testing ground" for various concepts). It was also the first Saturday series to be supplied by several different animation studios rather than a solitary supplier. Hanna-Barbera supplied the majority of the "movies," which were all animated and based on pre-established concepts that proved popular with kids. Such concepts were: *Tabitha and Adam, The Banana Splits, Oliver and the Artful Dodger, Robin Hoodnik, Yogi's Ark Lark, Gidget,* and *Lost in Space*. Other companies supplied *Popeye, The Red Baron, Willie Mays, Nanny and the Professor, That Girl,* and *Mad Mad Monsters*. Filmation had produced just one Superstar Movie but that one, the highest-rated of the series, was one of only two movies (Yogi being the other) which spawned its on series.

That movie *Lassie and the Spirit of Thunder Mountain* introduced us to the latest of the famous collie's ever-changing roster of masters: The Turner Family. They consisted of forest ranger Ben Turner, his wife Laura, their teenage children Jackie and Susan, and their youngest, Ben Jr., who although born blind (and being Saturday morning's first visually-challenged character) moved capably with Lassie as his guide. The Turners teamed up with their friend Gene Fox, a teenage Indian who lived at the nearby Thunder Mountain reservation, to stop a money-hungry congressman and a team of developers from destroying the Thunder Mountain National Park. During the adventure, Lassie ended up calling on several of the forest animals for assistance. Among the motley but surprisingly well-trained crew were an old mountain lion named Toothless, a raccoon named Robbie, a skunk named Rusty, a turtle ironically called Fastback, a rabbit called Babbitt, an owl named Groucho, Edgar the raven, and a prickly porcupine called Clyde. When the one-shot movie proved popular enough to spawn a weekly series, the animals were gathered into a formal group of almost-human (but for Saturday cartoons, still semi-realistic) squadron called the *Rescue Rangers* (a concept and name created some 15 years before Disney appropriated it for its Chip 'n Dale series) with Lassie serving as field leader under the Turners' guidance. In 15 episodes (with the previous season's *Superstar Movie* serving as the other two episodes with current wraparound footage), the Rangers undertook a wide variety of rescue missions, involving everything from Russian cosmonauts (with the Russian leader voiced by layout supervisor Les Kaluza, who had the thickest accent of anyone at the studio), to Navy frogmen. From helping a nearby town to endure a power blackout to stopping a mysterious "phantom" who was "haunting" a movie set. Their skills and reputations were such that a villain even created robot duplicates of the Rescue Rangers to rob a town.

After each episode a minute-long safety tip would follow. Jackie and Lassie hosted these public service announcements (PSA's). This season also brought the Filmation series into more family involvement as Lou Scheimer's son, Lane, his daughter, Erica, and director Hal Sutherland's son, Keith, began doing voices for various characters in their parent's series. The background music was written and composed by "Jeff Michael," a pseudonym for none-other than co-producer Norm Prescott.

LASSIE'S RESCUE RANGERS
☐ THE ANIMALS ARE MISSING
☐ MYSTIC MONSTER
☐ LASSIE SPECIAL
☐ THE IMPOSTERS
☐ DEADLY CARGO
☐ GRIZZLY
☐ DEEPSEA DISASTER
☐ BLACKOUT
☐ ARCTIC ADVENTURE
☐ THE SUNKEN GALLEON
☐ GOLDMINE
☐ RODEO
☐ HULLABALOO IN HOLLYWOOD
☐ TIDAL WAVE
☐ LOST

THE NEW ADVENTURES OF THE LONE RANGER

Broadcast Network History:
THE TARZAN / LONE RANGER ADVENTURE HOUR
Network Premiere: CBS, September, 1980, Saturday Mornings

Executive Producers: Lou Scheimer, Norm Prescott

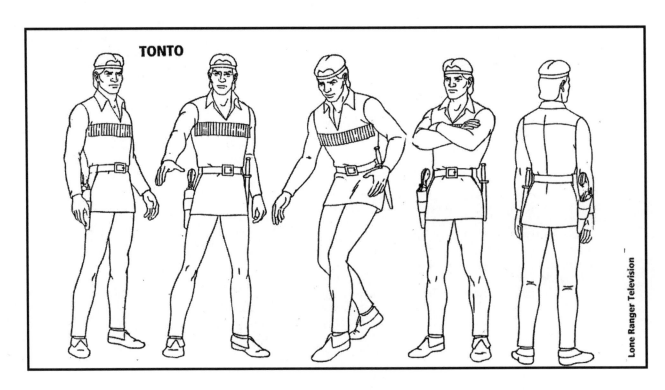

Principal Characters and Voices:
LONE RANGER..William Conrad
TONTO............................…….................……Ivan Naranjo

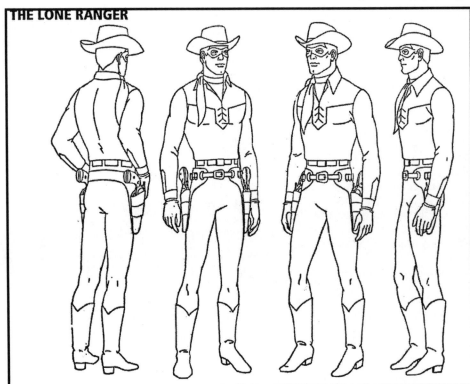

The Lone Ranger, Fran Striker's famed lawman, had previously starred in a long-running radio drama, which was followed by a successful live-action children series in the '50's. The "masked man" made his initial Saturday morning animated debut in a series for CBS that made up in its graphic screen style what it lacked in actual animation. The series, produced by famed animator Herb Klynn, combined the unique visual approach with *Wild, Wild West*-style adventure stories that brought all the action and gunplay of the western to the Saturday morning cartoon scene.

That was in 1966, when violence was much more acceptable to the animated menu than in 1980 when the network's Standards and Practices Departments (also known as censors) had long since banned fighting, gunplay, and many other violent acts that the censors felt kids could easily imitate.

So how did a series like *The Lone Ranger* end up onto CBS's schedule? For one thing, the series scored high ratings

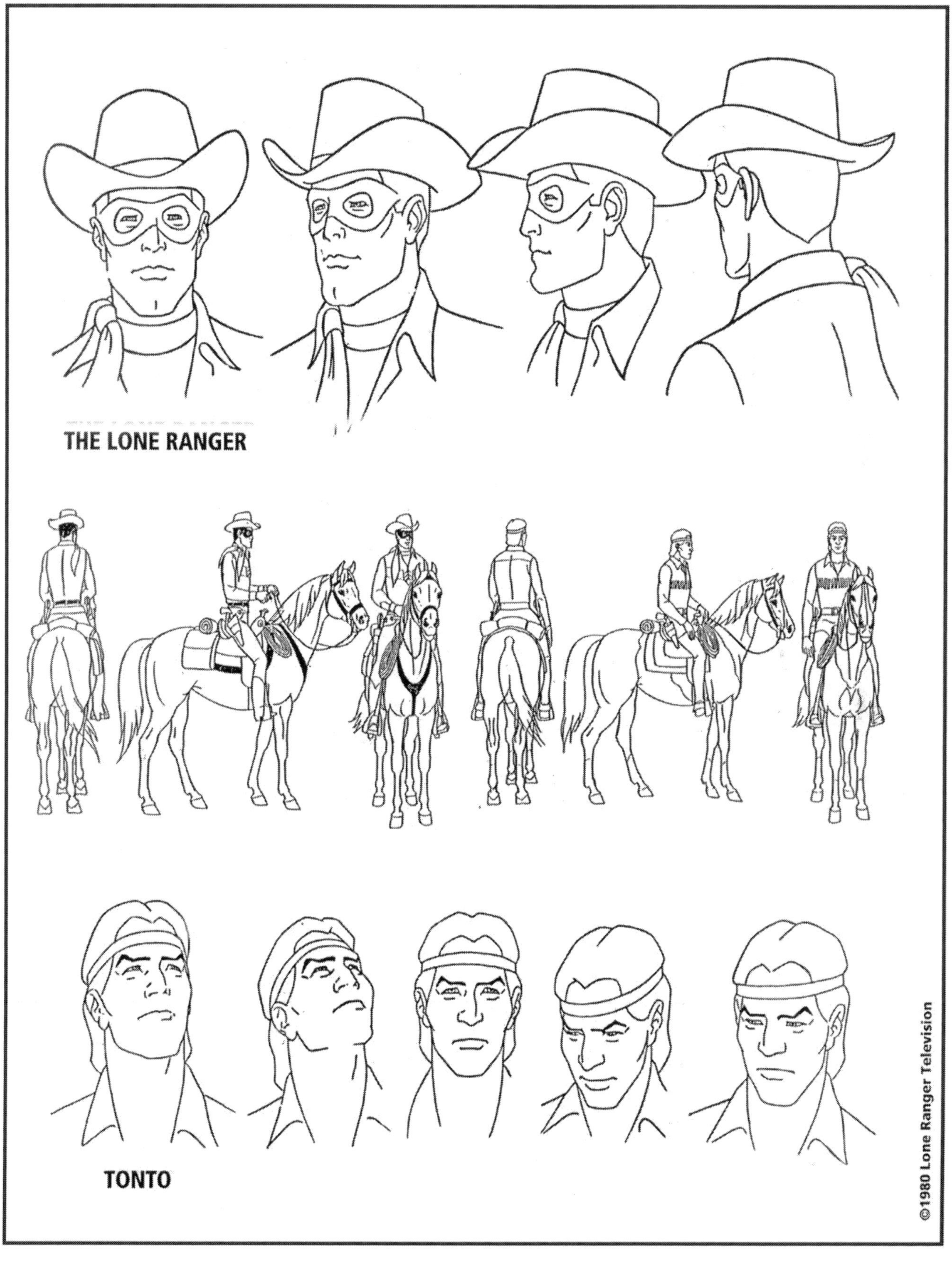

THE LONE RANGER

TONTO

©1980 Lone Ranger Television

when it originally ran in 1966. For another, Filmation knew that when they presented the new series to CBS, its' reputation for producing high quality, animated, non-violent adventure series would be a strong point in its favor (Filmation had first animated the character in a 1972 episode of *The Brady Kids* series: "Long Gone Silver," where the kids magical mynah bird, Marlon, uses a mixed-up magical spell to bring The Lone Ranger, Tonto, and Scout to the present…without materializing Silver!)

The hero also fit three of Filmation's other criteria: no super-powers, which made him a good match with their already-airing *Tarzan* series; a strong minority presence in the form of the Ranger's companion, Tonto; and Filmation's pro-educational stance, which was doubly served in this series. The stories were structured to have the masked man interact with famous historical figures of the time. Such figures included Nellie Bly, Wild Bill Hickok, President Ulysses S. Grant, and Fredrick Remington. In addition, each episode ended with an historical anecdote related by the Ranger or Tonto that reinforced the point of the story. As far as the gunplay in the series, the censors decided that while the Ranger could not shoot "baddies," he could shoot their guns out of their hands or do trick shots that would affect nearby objects—which would then affect the crooks.

Another strong point in the new series was the man selected to be the voice of The Lone Ranger. Nowadays, it's commonplace for celebrities to do voices for animated series, at the time this wasn't the case. So Filmation was delighted when famous actor William Conrad (*Jake and the Fatman, Cannon, Nero Wolf*) indicated his interest in providing his booming baritone to The Lone Ranger's speaking voice (this wasn't Conrad's first experience with cartoons; 20 years earlier he served a long period as the frantic, high-pitched narrator of *The Bullwinkle Show*). Conrad did want to hedge his bets somewhat, since he was working on various TV and movie projects at the time (and since there was that stigma about working on "cartoons"), so he agreed to portray The Lone Ranger on the condition that he be billed under a pseudonym. That name was "J. Darnoc,"

"Darnoc" being "Conrad" spelled backwards.

Originally produced as 16 half-hour episodes in its first season, the series was renewed for the following season as 16 eleven-minute, all-new segments. This allowed room for the incoming *Zorro* series. In 1980-1981, *The New Adventures of The Lone Ranger* were coupled with *Tarzan, Lord of the Jungle* to air as *The Tarzan/Lone Ranger Adventure Hour* later retitled *The Tarzan/Lone Ranger/Zorro Adventure Hour*.

THE LONE RANGER 1980
☐ RUNAWAY
☐ HANGA, THE NIGHT MONSTER
☐ THE YELLOWSTONE CONSPIRACY
☐ THE PRESIDENT PLOT
☐ THE GREAT BALLON RACE
☐ THE ESCAPE
☐ THE VALLEY OF GOLD
☐ TALL TIMBER
☐ BLOWOUT
☐ THE ABDUCTION OF TOM SAWYER
☐ THE BLACK MARE
☐ THE WILDEST WILD WEST SHOW
☐ THE SILVER MINE
☐ THE RENEGADE
☐ THE GREAT LAND RUSH
☐ THE MEMORY TRAP

1981
☐ HIGH AND DRY
☐ PHOTO FINISH
☐ THE GHOST WAGONS
☐ FRONT PAGE COVER-UP
☐ WALK A TIGHT ROPE
☐ UNNATURAL DISASTER
☐ SHOWDOWN ON THE MIDNIGHT QUEEN
☐ THE GREAT TRAIN TREACHERY
☐ BLAST-OUT
☐ THE LONG DRIVE
☐ RENEGADE ROUNDUP
☐ BANNING'S RAIDERS

THE NEW ADVENTURES OF MIGHTY MOUSE

Broadcast History:
Network Premiere: CBS, September, 1979, Saturday Morning

Syndicated History:
MIGHTY MOUSE AND FRIENDS
Fall, 1982

Executive Producers: Lou Scheimer, Norman Prescott
Producer: Don Christensen
Directors: Lou Zukor, Ed Friedman, Marsh La More, Gwen Wetzler, Kay Wright, Lou Kachivas
Writers: Buzz Dixon, Sam Simon, Ted Pedersen, Bill Danch, Jim Ryan, Coslough Johnson

Principal Characters and Voices:
MIGHTY MOUSE / OIL CAN HARRY ....
....Allan Oppenheimer
PEARL PUREHEART ....Diane Pershing.
HECKLE, JECKLE, QUACKULA......................Frank Welker
THEODORE E. BEAR ....Norm Prescott

Mighty Mouse was a propitious attempt to combine the wide appeal of two famed progenitors, Mickey Mouse and Superman. Artist Isidore Klein ignited the character's creation with an idea for a parody on Superman introduced in theatrical animated films in 1941. His concept involved a super fly, as he had read that the insect, for its size, possessed super strength. Instead, producer Paul Terry decided to make him a mouse; he had been partial to mice since his silent Farmer Al Falfa series and was undoubtedly influenced by the success of Mickey, to whom the character bore more than a passing resemblance at first. Premiering in "The Mouse of Tomorrow," October, 1942, the diminutive hero escaped from a brutal battle between cats and mice. He fled to a supermarket where he bathed in Super Soap, dined on Super Soup, dove into an enormous hunk of Super Cheese, and emerged as the red-caped Super Mouse. He had bulging biceps, a powerful chest that could repel bullets, and could fly like Superman. The all-powerful mite walked upright as a humanized rodent, and rescued not only his friends but Terry's studio as well. The renewal of Terrytoon's releasing contract with 20th Century-Fox Films looked bleak until the release of this cartoon, which rekindled their interest and led to a new pact, continuing production of the cartoons until the mid 1960's.

Serving as CBS' principal supplier during the late 1970's, due to their previous successes and due to a major falling out the network had with Hanna-Barbera, Filmation was handed the

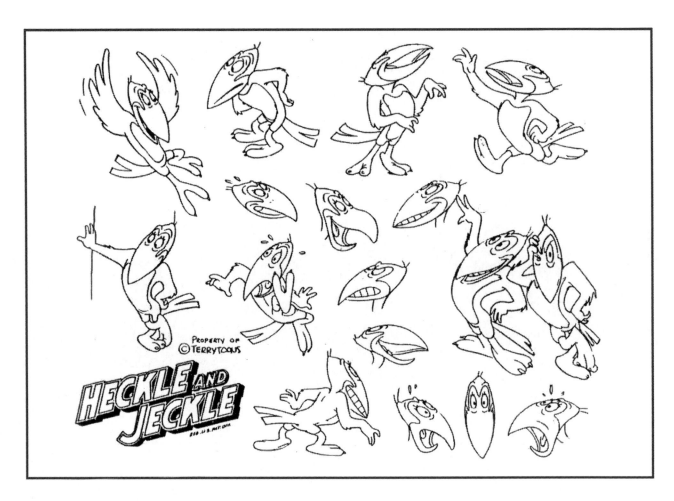

CBS-owned characters Mighty Mouse and Heckle and Jeckle, and an hour block of time to craft an all-new series.

In this new revived version, the cape-clad rodent once again defended mice minions everywhere and, in particular, extricated the beautiful Pearl Pureheart from the evil clutches of the conniving handle-bar mustached, Oil Can Harry and Swifty, his new bumbling henchman. The supermouse appeared in two episodic adventures in the hour-long format and a sixteen-chapter serial, *The Great Space Race*, featuring his arch foe and the southern-accented heroine as space invaders in a celestial cosmic chaos. Between segments the cartoon star, in *Mighty Mouse Environmental Bulletins*, provided cautions on wasting resources and littering. Heckle and Jeckle continued their magpie madness in a pair of supporting comedies while a sixth segment featured an original Filmation creation: the extremely obnoxious vampire mallard, "Quackula," made his debut. A cross between Daffy and Donald with fangs, the bloodthirsty duck slept in an egg-shaped coffin in the basement of a castle owned by a bear and terrorized his landlord and others. At least Filmation thought it was original; as it turned out, comic book artist Scott Shaw! had created a vampire duck of his own, Duckula, several years previously. Shaw! sued, and Filmation settled out of court and removed the character from network broadcast. The show returned and was reduced to half an hour in 1980-1981.

(*Author's Note:* Downplaying the violence in the original animated series for the new cartoon, Filmation instead played the series more for satire and slapstick humor. Accompanying this approach was a literal stretching of Filmation's artistic boundaries, influenced by the younger animation, stoyboard, and layout artist entering the studio that season. Producer Don Christensen taught a studio training program. Filmation's animation started showing more flexibility. The character's "takes" and "stretch and squash" became as prevalent as network censors would allow. Future Ralph Bakshi's Mighty Mouse artist Tom Minton, Eddie Fitzgerald, and John (Ren and Stimpy) Kricfalusi, peppered the shows with as much wildness as the "stodgy" Filmation could stand. Even this was not as much as they would have liked as Tom Minton later commented that the Bakshi's Mighty Mouse series was their "revenge" for what they could not do with the Filmation one.)

THE NEW ADVENTURES OF MIGHTY MOUSE
☐ MOUSETANKAMEN
☐ STOP-PAY TROLL
☐ THE TREASURE OF THE ILLO ARAMADA
☐ THE EXERCIST
☐ THE STAR OF CUCAMONGA

- ☐ GYPSY MICE
- ☐ LOCO MOTIVATIONS
- ☐ GANGMOUSE
- ☐ WINGS
- ☐ CATULA
- ☐ MOUSERACE
- ☐ NO TIME FOR LAUGHTER
- ☐ MOVIE MOUSE
- ☐ MIGHTY MOUSE MEETS MICK JAGUAR
- ☐ PHELINE OF THE ROCK OPERA
- ☐ CATTAN NEMO-OH-OH
- ☐ SNOW MOUSE
- ☐ HAUNTED HOUSE MOUSE
- ☐ CAT NESS MONSTER
- ☐ RUGGED RODENT
- ☐ DING DONG
- ☐ CATTENSTEIN
- ☐ CAT OF THE BASKERVILLES
- ☐ PEARL OF THE JUNGLE
- ☐ MOBY WHALE
- ☐ BIG TOP CAT
- ☐ THE DISORIENT EXPRESS
- ☐ THE MALTESE MOUSE
- ☐ BEAU JEST
- ☐ CURSE OF THE CAT
- ☐ AROUND THE WORLD IN 80 WAYS
- ☐ TUGBOAT PEARL

HECKLE AND JECKLE
- ☐ HECKLE AND JECKLE MEET GOLDFEATHER
- ☐ THE GOLDEN EGG
- ☐ THE HEROES
- ☐ CAVEBIRDS
- ☐ SHOW BUSINESS
- ☐ SPURS
- ☐ BIRDS OF PARADISE
- ☐ THE OPEN ROAD
- ☐ ROBOT FACTORY
- ☐ FARMER AND THE CROWS
- ☐ FOREIGN LEGION BIRDS
- ☐ MAIL BIRDS
- ☐ THE MALCON-TENTS
- ☐ BELLHOPS
- ☐ SPHINX!
- ☐ HANG TWO
- ☐ WITCH WAY OUTTA HERE?
- ☐ C.B. BIRDS
- ☐ SHOPPING CENTER
- ☐ WHERE THERE'S A WILL
- ☐ IDENTITY PROBLEM
- ☐ TIME WARPED
- ☐ INVISIBLE BIRDS

- ☐ MARATHON BIRDS
- ☐ SUPERMARKET
- ☐ WHEN KNIGHTHOOD WAS IN WEEDS

RIK
Miss Tickle's friend and co-guide through the world of magic.

MISS TICKLE
A magical Mary Poppins-like teacher who leads her students on wonderful adventures through an enchanted blackboard.

- ☐ ASTROBIRDS
- ☐ APARTMENT BIRDS
- ☐ IN THE 25TH CENTURY
- ☐ SAFARI BIRDS
- ☐ IN WONDERLAND
- ☐ ARABIAN NIGHTS AND DAYS

QUACKULA
- ☐ STAR BOARS
- ☐ HOUSE FOR SALE
- ☐ WEIRD BEAR
- ☐ MONSTER MASH
- ☐ UNCLE FERN
- ☐ THE MAGIC LAMP
- ☐ ROOM FOR RENT
- ☐ MORGANA LA DUCK
- ☐ RETURN OF THE STAR BOARS
- ☐ TIME AND BEFORE
- ☐ BUNGLED BURGLARY
- ☐ SHANGHAI SALTY
- ☐ PYRAMID
- ☐ HAUNTED HOUSE
- ☐ MAGIC DUCK
- ☐ THE FANTASTIC TWO-AND-A-HALF

MISSION: MAGIC!

Broadcast History:
Network Premiere: ABC, September, 1973, Saturday Mornings

Producers: Louis Scheimer, Norman Prescott

MISSION: MAGIC!

Director: Hal Sutherland
Writer: Marc Richards

Principal Characters and Voices:
RICK SPRINGFIELD..Himself
MISS TICKLE.......................................…..Lola Fisher
VINNIE / FRANKLIN ....….....Lane Scheimer
CAROL / KIM..............…...........................Erica Scheimer
SOCKS / HARVEY / MR. SAMUELS / TOLAMY (Rick's owl)
/ TUT-TUT (Tickle's Egyptian cat)....…....Howard Morris

After a couple of lean seasons, 1971 and 1972, the fall 1973 season was a bonanza for Filmation, as the studio reached another milestone. For the first time they had animated series on all three networks' Saturday morning schedules. Pro-social programming, which had combined entertainment with moralistic values, had caught on thanks to the previous season's *Fat Albert and the Cosby Kids* on rival CBS. ABC, noting this and their own ratings success with Filmation's *Brady Kids*, wanted a series, which would combine both elements.

Filmation's solution was *Mission Magic*, a concept which took TV teaching to a fantasy plane, first by featuring a school teacher as the lead character. This was Miss Tickle, a play on the word "mystical," a bespectacled schoolmarm whose purse contained a variety of magical gimmicks. She led a young group of "Archie-like" students who met each week under the after-school auspices of "The Adventures' Club," Brooklynese Vinnie, studious black student Franklin, malaproping Socks, fat and obnoxious Harv, oriental whiz kid Kim, and perky Carol.

Each week the six and Miss Tickle, when summoned by their friend who patrolled the "worlds beyond the blackboard" would, by using her magic, bring to life the stone statue of her Egyptian cat (she repeated the incantation, "Tut, Tut, a cat of ancient lore, it's time to draw the magic door," and the feline would spring to life). As Miss Trickle drew a "Magic Chalk Circle" on the blackboard, the portal widened to engulf the teacher and her young pupils into new adventures of historical fact. The adventurers traveled to a vast variety of fantastic worlds, from the past to the future, from under the sea to the subterranean. Moral values were inserted at the end of each episode, as the villains which the kids and Miss Tickle would encounter would usually reemphasize the educational point Miss Tickle was making in the class earlier in the story.

As noted earlier, this was for the most part Filmation's first totally original series to be produced for Saturday mornings. ABC, however wanted to hedge its bets, partly because the concept was so fanciful for Saturday mornings, and it wanted at least one character in the series to be based on a recognizable person. They decided on a pop musician who would be a perfect "contact" person for the kids to encounter, plus it would enable

them to add a rock music number in every episode of the show, a common practice at the time. ABC, realizing the prohibitive costs of such an endeavor, also noting the mixed success with their previous musical cartoon efforts, *The Jackson 5ive* (being largely a hit) and the next season's *The Osmonds* (not doing as well), decided that, rather than going for an already-established name, it might be better, and cheaper, to go for an up-and-comer with big-time breakout potential. ABC ran a poll/contest with several teen mags using several young singers to determine who would be the "possible superstar of tomorrow." The winner was a young Australian singer/songwriter, Rick Springfield, who won over 400 others. Animated Rick then became the contest man who patrolled "the worlds beyond the blackboard," summoning Miss Tickle and the Adventures Club via his magical gramaphone. Rick not only provided the likeness and his Aussie-accented voice to the character, but also wrote the 15 songs and the title tune used for the series. One song he did not sing; it was sung by Miss Tickle, whose voice artist Lola Fisher was also an accomplished singer.

Springfield's career, post-teen idolatry, has been interesting, as he starred in the soap-opera *General Hospital* for several years and is starring in the new ABC adventure series *Human Target*…minus the Australian accent which he has managed to lose over the intervening years. In fact, he almost never mentions that he did this animation job twenty years ago, figuring that it would be forgotten by this time.

Since Filmation had lost the rights to the character as "Rick Springfield," but the character wears a white jumpsuit with an "R" on the chest, all references to his last name were edited out and renamed "Rik."

To further give the show a strong sendoff, Miss Tickle starred in a crossover episode with the show that aired before it, The Brady Kids, as it was established that Miss Tickle and The Brady Kids' Marlon had previous…dealings. Despite this, the show only ran a single season on ABC.

MISSION: MAGIC!
☐ THE LAND OF BACKWARDS
☐ MODRAN
☐ DISSONIA
☐ LAND OF HYDE AND GOSEEK
☐ THE CITY INSIDE THE EARTH 2600 A.D.
☐ SOMETHING FISHY
☐ GIANT STEPPES
☐ STATUE OF LIMITATIONS
☐ WILL THE REAL RICK SPRINGFIELD, PLEASE STAND UP?
☐ DOCTOR ASTRO
☐ DOCTOR DAGUERROTYPE
☐ NEPHREN
☐ MODRAN RETURNS
☐ HORSE FEATHERS
☐ A LIGHT MYSTERY

MY FAVORITE MARTIANS

Broadcast History:
NetworkPremiere: CBS, September, 1973,Saturday Mornings

Syndicated History:
THE GROOVIE GOOLIES AND FRIENDS
Producers: Lou Scheimer, Norm Prescott
Director: Hal Sutherland
Animation Directors: Don Towsley, Rudy Larriva, Bill Reed, Lou Zukor

Principal Characters and Voices
UNCLE MARTIN ....Jonathan Harris
ANDROMEDA ("ANDY")…..….......................Lane Scheimer
KATY O'HARA / LORELEI BROWN / JAN CORAL / MISS CASSEROLE…... Jane Webb

TIM O'HARA / BRAD BRENNAN / SECURITY OFFICER BRENNAN / TINY / CRUMBS / CHUMP (Brad's pet chimpanzee) / OKIE ("Andy's" Martian dog)..................………
....Howard Morris

My Favorite Martian was a prime-time live-action situation comedy and a moderate hit for CBS during its three-season run 1963-1966. The series starred Ray Walston as the Martian and Bill Bixby, later to star in *The Incredible Hulk* series, as the Martian's "nephew," Tim. The series dealt with the misadventures of the Martian pretending to be a normal Earthling and living with Tim while trying to fix his wrecked spaceship so that he could finally go back to Mars.

In the last episode of that series, a new character was introduced: Martin's Martian nephew, Andromeda, who also crash-landed on Earth. If the series had not been cancelled, "Andy" would have become a regular character in the sci-fi sitcom, as he too would be trying to get back to Mars and pretend to be a normal "all-American teenager" in the process.

The addition of an animated version of his sci-fi sitcom to CBS' Saturday morning schedule in 1973 gave series creator Jack Chertog the choice to do with his new character that was denied with the live-action series' cancellation, since CBS that season was high on teenaged kids' versions of previous hit sitcoms; they had also commissioned an animated teenaged Jeannie series from Hanna-Barbera. Chertog's future "Martian" plans fit perfectly with what CBS wanted.

Added to the animated series *My Favorite Martians,* with Martin, Tim, Andy, and their landlord Mrs. Brown, were Andy's teenage "cousin" Katy, their school friends Tiny, Crumbs, Jan, Coral, and teacher Miss Casserole. They concealed their damaged spacecraft in Tim's garage. Also from the red planet was Andy's dog Okie Dokie, a pink shaggy creature with antennae. Passing them off as "normal," Tim's problems began when the Martians displayed their extra-terrestrial powers. Andy was enrolled in Katy's high school, where his superior intellect made him suspect.

Mr. Brennan, a minor character in the original live-action series, became Security Officer Brennan, a major pain-in-the-neck for the O'Haras, as his only "security" job seemed to be snooping on those "weird Martian-birds" that lived upstairs. As much of a pain as Brennan was to Martin, a new teenaged character, Brad Brennan, son of Officer Brennan, was to Andy and Katy. Likewise, his pet Chump the Chimp was a pain to Okie Dokie.

The series benefited from the multitudinous vocal talents

of Howard Morris, who played all the male characters with the exception of Martin and Andy and all the animals. Also of great import was Jonathan Harris, who segued from portraying the villainous clown "Dr. Zachary Smith" in the Live-action sci-fi series *Lost in Space* to the first in a series of fruitful roles for Filmation, culminating in his later starring in two live-action series for the studio, *Uncle Croc's Block* and *Space Academy*.

MY FAVORITE MARTIANS
- ☐ CHECK UP
- ☐ LIFE STYLE
- ☐ HOME SCHTICK
- ☐ WALL TO WALL FLOWER
- ☐ THE CLEO CAPER
- ☐ ROBOT TAILOR
- ☐ LONELY OKIE?
- ☐ TRIPLE TROUBLE
- ☐ THE INCREDIBLE SHRINKING SHIP
- ☐ MY FAVORITE NEIGHBOR
- ☐ ALLERGY
- ☐ TRUANT TEACHER
- ☐ LOVE : MARTIAN STYLE
- ☐ THE CHUMP WHO CRIED CHIMP
- ☐ CREDIBILITY GAP
- ☐ GARAGE SALE

SABRINA THE TEENAGE WITCH

Broadcast History:
THE ARCHIE COMEDY HOUR
Network Premiere: CBS, September, 1969
Mornings

Producers: Norm Prescott, Lou Schiemer
Director: Hal Sutherland
Art Director: Don Christensen
Writers: Bob Ogle, Jim Mulligan, Jim Ryan, Bill Danch, Jack Mendelson, Chuck Menville

THE NEW ARCHIE / SABRINA HOUR
Network Premiere: NBC, September 1977, Saturday Mornings

Executive Producers: Norm Prescott, Lou Schiemer
Producer: Don Christensen
Director: Marsh Lamore, Don Towsley, Rudy Larriva
Associate Producers / Story Editors: Jim Ryan, Bill Danch

SUPER WITCH THE BANG-SHANG LALAPALOOZA SHOW
Network Premiere: NBC, November 1977, Saturday Mornings

Executive Producers: Lou Scheimer, Norm Prescott
Producer: Hal Sutherland
Creative Director: Don Christensen
Directors: Don Towsley, Lou Zukor, Rudy Larriva, Bill Reed

Principal Characters:
ARCHIE ANDREWS / HOT DOG / MR. WEATHERBEE / COACH CLEATS / CHUCK / COUSIN AMBROSE / CHIEF / MR. ANDREWS / MR. LODGE / SALEM CHILI DOG.......
....Dallas McKennon
JUGHEAD JONES / BIG MOOSE / POPS / FRANKIE / WOLFIE / MUMMY / GHOULAHAND / HOT DOG JR........
....Howard Morris
BETTY COOPER / VERONICA LODGE / BIG ETHEL / MISS GRUNDY / SABRINA / AUNT HILDA / AUNT ZELDA / HAGATHA / BELLA LA GHOSTLY.....Jane Webb
REGGIE MANTLE ....John Erwin
COUNT DRAC / BATSO / GOOLIHAND............Larry Storch
CARLOS...Jose Flores

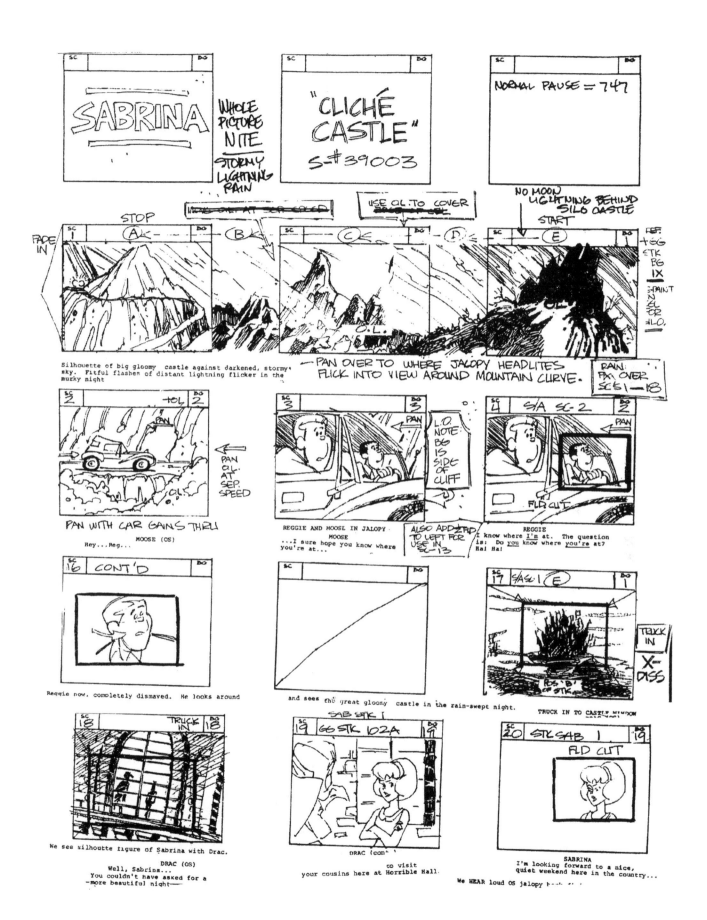

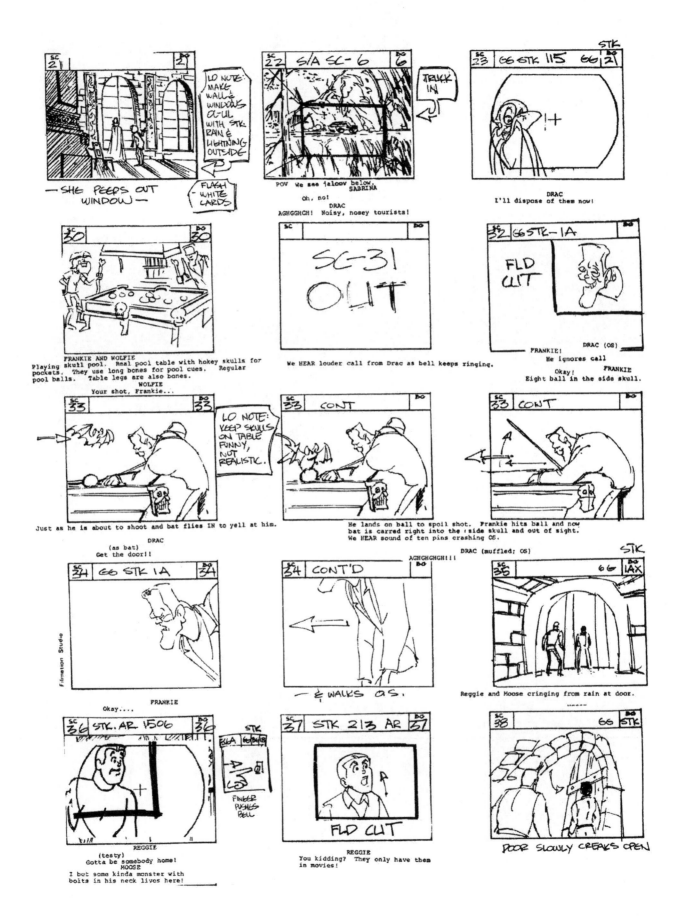

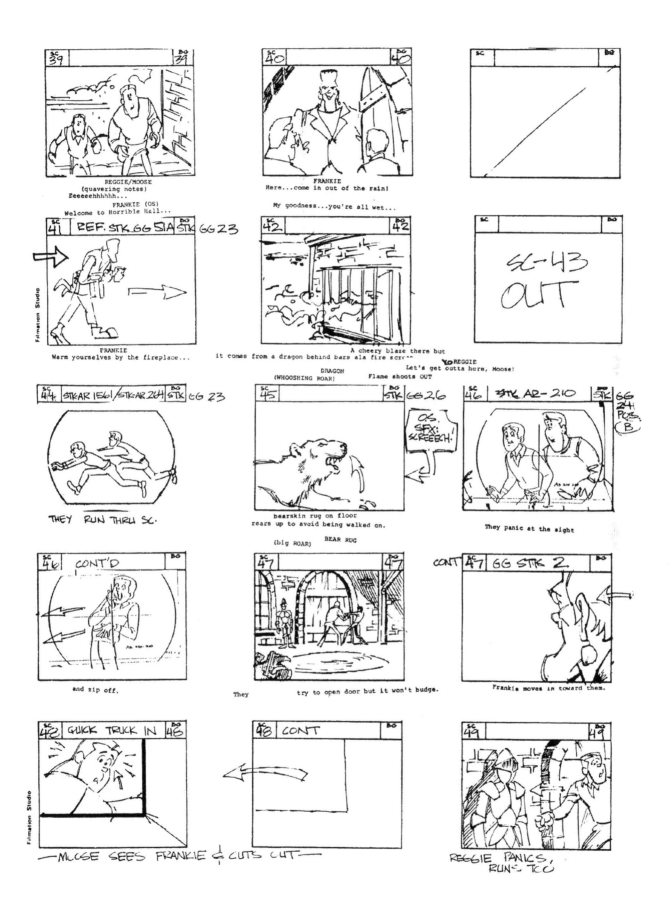

Sabrina, the Teen-Age Witch, graduated from *The Archie Comedy Hour* (but fortunately not from Riverdale High) into her own hour-length series on CBS the following season (1970) teamed with new Filmation-created characters, *The Groovie Goolies*.

Sabrina, herself a Filmation-created addition to the established Archie series, was inspired by CBS children's head Fred Silverman noticing that one of the highest-rated series among kids was rival network ABC's prime-time Bewitched live-actioner. That series, which featured a family of witches, impressed him enough to where he briefly entertained the idea of commissioning a possible animated version of it for CBS. This was, of course, before he decided to not put a show with another network's characters on his network. Instead, Silverman and Filmation brainstormed and spawned Sabrina. The comedy dealt with the exploits of Sabrina, a comely teenager, her pet cat Salem, and her two aunts: stern aunt Hilda and bubbly aunt Zelda, new residents to Riverdale. All were secretly witches, although Sabrina downplayed the use of her magic, wanting to live like a normal teenager. It was because of this attitude that her aunts (and head witch Miss Della) always reprimanded Sabrina for not keeping up with her "hexwork." Her character frequently interacted with the Archie's gang, all of whom were unaware that there was a witch in their midst…with the annoying exception of Reggie, who was bound and determined to expose Sabrina and her aunts to everyone as the witches they were. His character continually schemed to bring this about.

The rating's success of *The Archie's Comedy Hour* (itself a spin-off of the previous season's smash-hit *Archie Show*) had Silverman deciding to spread the wealth throughout his Saturday morning schedule by spinning off the two Sabrina segments in *The Archie Comedy Hour* into its own series. Uncertain that Sabrina could carry an entire half-hour, let alone the hour-length series that he had envisioned, Silverman put the Filmation braintrust to work on conceiving a new set of characters and situations outside of the Archie gang for her to cavort in.

Those characters turned out to be comedic plays on various Hollywood movie monsters, now hipper and wackier as the Groovie Goolies. These new lead characters were Frankie (based on the Frankenstein monster), a big, dumb, and lovable lug named Count Drac (based on Dracula, this vapid vampire literally hit the ground to become a bat), and Wolfie (who owed as much to radio personality Wolfman Jack as to the movie's Wolfman…an overgrown beach-bum). The Goolies shared the stage and locale of Horrible Hall, situated just outside of Riverdale, with a whole tribe of freaky characters…all related (cousins) to Sabrina and her aunts. Among those characters were the Mummy, the one-handed Goolihand, gossipy Bella La Ghostly, spellcasting Aunt Hagatha, and the two-headed Doctors Jekyll and Hyde, who constantly beat each other over the head (no pun intended) about everything.

The Goolies co-starred with Sabrina and the Archie gang in comedy capers as well as their own joke-telling and skit segments. Frankie, Wolfie, and Count Drac also formed The Groovie Goolies pop group, singing a new song each week (they

actually released an album on RCA Records). Other musical sequences appeared each week which were provided by several other "musical groups:" The Mummies and the Puppies, The Spirits of '76, The Rolling Headstones, and The Bare Bones Band. "Chic-A-Boom" was a top ten chart hit, which brought new teenage viewers to this "kids" show

The following season (1971), Sabrina and the Goolies were split into their own half-hours that aired on Sundays. A year later, Filmation established a deal with Warner Brothers: Filmation would produce (and Warner Brothers would distribute) low-budget animated features and, in turn, Filmation would gain access to certain Warner characters. The end result was the *ABC Saturday Morning Superstar Movie: Daffy Duck and Porky Pig Meet The Groovie Goolies,* in which the Goolies set off to Hollywood to meet their favorite Warners' animal characters, who were making a movie that was being "haunted" by the "Phantom of the Flickers." Included in this movie/pilot was a live-action/stop-motion sequence in which Frankie, Wolfie, Drac, and Hauntleroy became live-action characters cavorting in a western town. The Goolies were later renamed the Super Fiends in a planned move to add them to the failing *Uncle Croc's Block* series running on ABC during the 1975-76 season. However, ABC, noting the series' overall low ratings, decided to jettison the series from the network before this happened. *The Groovie Goolies*, packaged with several other Filmation series, hit the syndication in 1977 as *The Groovie Goolies and Friends.*

THE NEW SABRINA
- [ ] HAIR TODAY - GONE TOMORROW
- [ ] A WITCH IN TIME
- [ ] WHEN THE CAT'S AWAY
- [ ] COSTUME PARTY
- [ ] LET'S HAVE A HAND FOR JUGHEAD
- [ ] THE NEW FREEWAY
- [ ] BLUE WHALE
- [ ] FOOTBALL GAME
- [ ] TOWN BEAUTIFUL
- [ ] HORSE'S MOUTH
- [ ] BIRDMAN OF RIVERDALE
- [ ] HOEDOWN SHOWDOWN
- [ ] SPOOKY SPOKES
- [ ] YOU OUGHTA BE IN PICTURES
- [ ] THE GENERATION FLAP
- [ ] SCHOOL DAZE
- [ ] UG AT THE BAT
- [ ] COMPUTERIZED MOOSE
- [ ] ROSE-COLORED GLASSES
- [ ] LIVING DOLLS
- [ ] CAKE BAKE
- [ ] HOT ROD DERBY THE BEAR FACTS
- [ ] CHILD CARE
- [ ] WITCHES GOLD OPEN
- [ ] RUMMAGE SALE
- [ ] HIGH SCHOOL DROP-INS
- [ ] BIG DEAL
- [ ] FRANKIE
- [ ] BEACHED
- [ ] OUCH
- [ ] SMOG
- [ ] DIRTY POOL
- [ ] THE GRAYED OUTDOORS
- [ ] SHORT CHANGED
- [ ] MIS-GUIDED TOUR

- ☐ THAT OLD TRACK MAGIC
- ☐ MOOSE'S ALTER-FALTER
- ☐ MORTAL TERROR
- ☐ WEATHER OR NOT
- ☐ FLYING SORCERY

SHE-RA, PRINCESS OF POWER

Broadcast History:
Syndication Premiere:
September, 1985

Cable Premiere: USA September, 1989

Executive Producer: Lou Scheimer
Directors: Lou Kachivas, Ed Friedman, Marsh La More, Mark Glamack, Tom Sito, Richard Trueblood
Writers: Larry Ditillio, Don Heckman, Francis Moss, Harvey Brenner, Michael Utvich, Don Heckman, Michael Chase Walker, J. Michale Stracynski
Character Design: Herb Hazelton, Diane Keeler

Principal Characters and Voices:
MADAME RAXX / SHE-RA / FROSTA	Melendy Britt
BOW / HORDAK	George Dicenzo
CASTASPELLA / GLIMMER / SHADOW WEAVER / CATRA	Linda Gary
IMP	Erica Scheimer
LIGHTHOPE / SPRINT / SWIFTWIND / HORDE SOLIDERS / LOO-KEE	Lou Scheimer
KOWL / MANTENNA / LEECH	Erik Gumden
BROOM / HE-MAN	John Erwin
SKELETOR	Alan Oppenheimer

A curious thing happened during the meteoric rise in sales of the *He-Man and the Master of the Universe* toy line…even though it was marketed and sold mainly to young boys, Mattel Toy's market tracking showed an unusual percentage of sales to young girls. It was further realized that the girls showed an affinity to the two "women's" figures in the He-Man toy line: the heroic Tee-La and the villainous Evil-Lyn. It was also realized that they liked playing with these two characters alongside their male counterparts. Sensing a potential sales windfall in this, Mattel Toys and Filmation sat down to develop what at the time were the first female action figures—as an adjunct to the He-Man toy line.

Setting the series on Etheria, a parallel world to He-Man's Eternia, *She-Ra, Princess of Power* focused on Adora, He-Man's heretofore-unknown twin sister, who, not knowing of her royal heritage, served as the leader of main Etheria bad-guy Hordak's troops (Hordak also had a linkage to the toy line…he was Skeletor's teacher at one time. Unlike Skeletor though, who consistently strove to conquer Eternia, Hordak had conquered Etheria). After a fateful meeting with brother Adam, Adora learned of her true heritage and claimed her share of the power of Grayskull, which transformed her into the super-powerful She-Ra.

She-Ra possessed super-strength, healing powers, and a heightened sensibility to nature. Her horse, Spirit, was, when she pointed her power-sword toward the animal, transformed into the flying swiftwind. In addition, her sword, unlike He-Man's, could be transformed into various other weapons, including a shield, a rope, or once even a space-helmet. Breaking from Hordak, Adora then lead the main group of rebels opposing Hordak. Among those rebels were the arrow-shooting Bow (with Hordak, one of the few male characters in the cast), the magical Castaspella,

SHE-RA STORYBOARD TRANSFERMATION BY KEITH TUCKER

her daughter Glimmer, the frigidity-casting Frosta, the imperious Kowl, and the somewhat-wacky Madame Razz. Battles were constantly fought between the rag-tag rebels and Hordak's forces which included the sinister spellcaster Shadow Weaver, the snarling Katra, the dopey duo Leech and Mantanna, and Hordak's favorite…the odious little Imp. Skeletor made frequent forays into Etheria to cause trouble, which also necessitated frequent appearances from big brother He-Man on the show as well. The series ran for 65 half-hours in 1985 and had received a 28 episode order for the next two seasons; however, the total failure of the She-Ra toy line caused the cancellation of the second 14 episodes. A new hour-length Christmas special was produced however, and it featured the combined casts from both *He-Man* and *She-Ra*.

The pre-requisite Filmation moral segment at the end of each show was delivered by a little character using a gimmick that predated *Where's Waldo* by several years. The character, appropriately named "Loo-Kee," delivered the morals after first challenging the audience to find where he had been hiding in the background earlier in the story. In a copycat notion similar to Hasbro's *Transformers*/Tonka's *GoBots*, the Galoob toy company decided to create a similar toyline to *She-Ra: the Golden Girls* female action line. Unfortunately, despite an allegiance with competing animation house Ruby-Spears, Galoob didn't have the financial clout to launch an animated series like She-Ra's, and the failure of both toy lines chilled the toy market on doing female action figures (even female characters in male action figure toy lines) for years to come.

SHE-RA, PRINCESS OF POWER
☐ INTO ETHERIA
☐ BEAST ISLAND
☐ SHERA UNCHAINED
☐ REUNIONS
☐ BATTLE FOR BRIGHT MOON
☐ DUEL AT DEVLAN
☐ THE SEA HAWK
☐ THE RED KNIGHT
☐ THE MISSING AX
☐ THE PRISONERS OF BEAST ISLAND
☐ THE PERILS OF THE WHISPERING WOODS
☐ THE LAUGHING DRAGON
☐ KING MIRO'S JOURNEY
☐ FRIENDSHIP
☐ HE AIN'T HEAVY

©1985 Mattel, Filmation

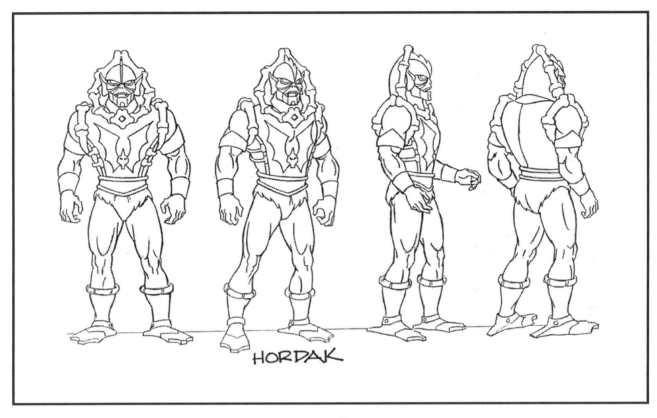

HORDAK

- RETURN OF THE SEA HAWK
- LOSS FOR WORDS
- HORDE PRIME TAKES A HOLIDAY
- THE ENCHANTED CASTLE
- THREE COURAGEOUS HEARTS
- THE STONE IN THE SWORD
- THE CRYSTAL CASTLE
- THE CROWN OF KNOWLEDGE
- THE MINES OF MONDOR
- SMALL PROBLEMS
- BOOK BURNING
- THE ELDRITCH MIST
- BOW'S FAREWELL
- THE PRICE OF FREEDOM
- PLAY IT AGAIN, BOW
- THE RELUCTANT WIZARD
- FRIENDS ARE WHERE YOU FIND THEM
- A TALENT FOR TROUBLE
- TROLL'S DREAM
- GATEWAY TO TROUBLE
- THE UNICORN KING
- THE ANXIOUS APPRENTICE
- ZOO STORY
- INTO THE DARK DIMENSION
- TREASURE OF THE FIRST ONES
- GLIMMER'S STORY
- ENEMY WITH MY FACE
- WELCOME BACK KOWL
- THE ROCK PEOPLE
- HUNTRA
- MICAH OF BRIGHT MOON
- THE PRINCE OF POWER
- BIRDS OF A FEATHER
- FOR WANT OF A HORSE
- JUST LIKE ME
- MY FRIEND, MY ENEMY
- THE WIZARD
- UNEXPECTED ALLY
- THE LIGHT OF THE CRYSTAL
- LOO KEE LENDS A HAND
- OF SHADOWS AND SKULLS
- JUNGLE FEVER
- BLACK SNOW
- ANCHORS ALOFT (PART I - II)

- ☐ DARKSMOKE AND FIRE
- ☐ MAGICATS
- ☐ UNEXPECTED ALLY
- ☐ WILD CHILD
- ☐ THE GREATEST MAGIC

SPACE SENTINELS
(formerly THE YOUNG SENTINELS)

Broadcast History:
Network Premiere: NBC, September, 1977, Saturday Morning

Executive Producers: Louis Scheimer, Norman Prescott
Producer: Don Christensen
Director: Hal Sutherland
Writers: J. Michael Reaves, Kathleen Barnes, Jerry Winnick, Donald F. Gult, David Wise

Principal Characters and Voices:
ASTRAEA	Dee Timberlake
HERCULES / SENTINEL ONE	George DiCenzo
MERCURY	Evan Kim
M.O.	Ross Hagen

Developed during the spring of 1977 and sold for a debut to NBC that fall, *The Young Sentinels,* although fitting into the category of a rare Filmation original series, reflected a number of influences and derivations in its execution. Its major outside influence (which was evident in many other series of that time) was that spring's smash hit movie, *Star Wars,* which in turn made its presence felt in the series' approach to technology (an intricacy in the backgrounds, especially the spaceship interiors, that hadn't been approached by Filmation's artists before). A prime example of this can be seen in one of the supporting characters, the maintenance operator M.O., who reflected the "cute robot" approach popularized by *Star War's* droids R2-D2 and C-3PO (other Filmation characters afflicted by this approach were Archie's "Q," *Space Academy's* "Beepo," and *Star Command's* "Twiki").

M.O. served as robotic assistant to the computerized lifeform known as Sentinel One which, ages before, had pulled three humans from various ancient Earth cultures and brought them to a faraway world. It was on this world where Sentinel One imbued the youths with super-powers before returning them to Earth aboard his spaceship which landed within a dormant volcano. There, their exploits earned them the status of the Earthly legends that they were named after: the blonde haired Hercules, who had the strength of a hundred men; the oriental Mercury, who could move at the speed of light; and Astraea, the black female leader of the team who could transform into any animal guise (the interracial makeup of the team was at the time unusual…even more so by making the black woman the leader, but to Filmation's credit, they constantly strove to create more minority characters in their series…often without network prodding).

Despite (or perhaps, because of) rather challenging scripts, the ratings on the series when it premiered were low enough that NBC, seeking a "stylistic link-up" with the Filmation-produced CBS rival *Space Academy,* changed the series' name to The Space Sentinels later that season. It didn't help, and after only one season the series was canceled. However, part of the show did live on to the next season as Hercules became one of CBS' *Freedom Force* characters. in that season's *Tarzan and the Super 7.*

SPACE SENTINELS
- ☐ MORPHEUS, THE SINISTER SENTINEL
- ☐ SPACE GIANTS

SPACE SENTINELS

ASTREA

MERCURY

HERCULES

©1977 Filmation

- ☐ THE TIME TRAVELER
- ☐ THE SORCERESS
- ☐ THE RETURN OF ANUBIS
- ☐ THE WIZARD OF ODD
- ☐ THE PRIME SENTINEL
- ☐ COMMANDER NEMO
- ☐ VOYAGE TO THE INNER WORLD
- ☐ LOKI
- ☐ FAUNA
- ☐ THE JUPITER SPORE
- ☐ THE WORLDSHIP

SPORT BILLY

Broadcast History:
European Broadcast Premiere: September, 1982
American Network Premiere: NBC February, 1984
Saturday Mornings

Executive Producers: Norm Prescott, Lou Scheimer

Principal Characters/Voices:
SPORT BILLY .... Lane Scheimer
EVIL QUEEN .... Linda Gary

With Filmation's animated fare now being broadcast and syndicated all over the world, the studio's reputation and fame had grown to such an extent that they were soon given a rare and unique opportunity...to produce an American-made animated series for a non-American market place. This happened when the company was commissioned by a West German sports combine to create and produce an animated series centered on their company mascot, Sport Billy. The character was already as famous in Germany as Mickey Mouse was in America.

The series Filmation conceived, Sport Billy, featuring the sweats-attired boy mascot as a time-traveling superhero from another planet who is assigned by his world's leaders for a special mission: to prevent a villainous queen from ruining sports all over the Earth. Armed with his amazing Omni-Sack (from which Billy could pull out anything from a pencil to a phone booth) the hero, with his pet dog companion, chased the queen through various time-periods and historical places. They also encountered famous figures during their tempestuous time treks. Billy emphasized sportsmanship and teamwork in each of his episodes. These were presented both in the stories and in a traditional Filmation trademark particularly admired by the Germans, with a non-lip synced song sequence at each episode's end.

The sixteen half-hours were produced and were originally supposed to be broadcast in Europe. But NBC (in need of some rapid mid-season replacement programming for their Saturday morning schedule in 1984) made a deal with Filmation to bring the series to America for broadcast here. This was thanks to the fact that even though Sport Billy was produced for German audiences...it was an English-language show.

SPORT BILLY (1979)
- ☐ JOUST IN TIME
- ☐ TROUBLE IN TOKYO
- ☐ MEXICAN HOILDAY
- ☐ RETURN TO OLYMPUS
- ☐ CHINESE PUZZLE
- ☐ TEAMWORK
- ☐ BAD WEATHER BLUES
- ☐ A VICE IN THE WILDERNESS
- ☐ WHEEL OF FORTUNE
- ☐ HYDE AND SEEK
- ☐ POWER OF THE OMNISAC
- ☐ A RACE IN SPACE
- ☐ TRIAL BY FIRE
- ☐ THE GREAT TEXAS HOLE-IN-ONE
- ☐ ARABIAN NIGHTS AND DAYS
- ☐ MIXED DOUBLES

(1980)
- ☐ VIKING FOR A DAY
- ☐ MONSTER FROM THE LOCH
- ☐ MYSTERY OF THE RUSSIAN CAVE
- ☐ RAH! RAH! BILLY!
- ☐ PERIL IN PERU
- ☐ ATHENIAN ADVENTURE
- ☐ PURE LUCK
- ☐ TAJ MAHAL MYSTERY
- ☐ AUSTRALIAN ADVENTURE
- ☐ A TALE OF TWO BILLYS

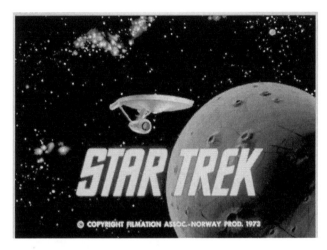

STAR TREK

BROADCAST HISTORY:
First Telecast:
NBC Saturday Mornings, September 8, 1973 - August 30, 1975

Original Run:
NBC Saturday 10:30 - 11:00 AM   Sep. 1973 - Dec. 1973
NBC Saturday 11:00 - 11:30 AM   Jan. 1974 - Aug. 1974
NBC Saturday 11:30 AM - Noon   Sep. 1974 - Aug. 1975

Syndication:
Nickelodeon Saturday 6:30 - 7:00 PM   Sep. 1984 - ? 1988
Sci-Fi Channel Sunday 6:30 - 7:00 AM   Oct. 1992 - Mar. 1993
Sci-Fi Channel Sunday 9:30 - 10:00 AM   Apr. 1993 - Dec. 1993
Sci-Fi Channel Saturday 10:30 - 11:00 AM   Jan. 1994 - Mar. 1994
TV Land Saturday 12:30 - 1:00 PM   April 1999 - December 1999

Producers: Lou Scheimer, Norm Prescott
Director: Hal Sutherland
Associate Producer: Dorothy ("D.C.") Fontana
Art Director: Don Christensen
Writers: D.C. Fontana, Marc Daniels, Margaret Armen, David Gerrold, James Schmerer, Walter Koenig

Principal Characters:

CAPTAIN JAMES T. KIRK............William Shatner
SCIENCE OFFICER SPOCK........Leonard Nimoy
DOCTOR LEONARD McCOY....DeForest Kelley
CHIEF ENGINEER MONTGOMERY
SCOTT/LIEUTENANT AREX.......James Doohan
LIEUTENANT UHURA...............Nichelle Nichols
LIEUTENANT SULU......................George Takei
NURSE CHRISTINE CHAPEL /
LIEUTENANT M'RESS...................Majel Barrett

Throughout the 1980's and into the 1990's, the Star Trek phenomena re-emerged as a successful string of motion pictures. This was due to the increasing demand for further Star Trek adventures after the original show had found its audience in syndication… which followed its initial demise after an unsuccessful three-year network run. Not widely attributed to the resurfacing of Star Trek was Filmation's animated series, which ran in the early '70's. Gathering the vocal talents of the original performers, the crew of the starship Enterprise was reunited for further adventures during its five-year mission exploring the unknown vastness of the final frontier.

During the period between the original and animated series, the property (owned by Paramount pictures) had remained in production limbo. Having always appreciated the original series, Filmation's Lou Scheimer felt that the show might enjoy an animated second coming on Saturday mornings. Though other production companies sought the rights to produce an animated Star Trek, Scheimer was lucky enough to obtain them—provided that Star Trek creator Gene Roddenberry garnished creative control. Roddenberry also insisted that D.C. Fontana serve as not only the new show's story editor (as she did on the original series) but that she assume the duties of associate producer as

miere episode "Yesteryear," which is usually heralded as the animated show's finest episode). The result was in what Scheimer refers to as "one of the smoothest operations we (Filmation) ever had."

Filmation had a 22 episode/two-year commitment to the show, with the entire cast (save Walter "Chekov" Koenig, who contributed in writing only with "The Infinite Vulcan") reuniting together for the first time in a work-related atmosphere since shooting the last episode of the original live-action series. Although it is commonly believed that the actors recorded their voices separately and at their convenience, William Shatner, Leonard Nimoy, DeForest Kelley, and the rest of the cast voiced the majority of the episodes as an ensemble at the recording studio. While the principal cast members stuck to voicing their characters exclusively, others with lesser roles (James Doohan, Nichelle Nichols, George Takei, and Majel Barrett) provided voices for the majority of guest characters as well as the extraneous plethora of ship personnel.

Budgeted at $75,000 per episode, the animated Trek also allowed writers from the original show to pen new adventures for the Enterprise crew. In some cases, writers returned to script "sequels" to their previous live-action counterparts. Famed Trek episode "The Trouble with the Tribbles" gave way to the animated "More Tribbles With Troubles," both scripted by David Gerrold. The same went for the animated "Mudd's Passion" written by original Trek writer and "Mudd" creator Stephen Kandel. Both of those episodes brought back original guest stars to furnish the vocal talents they had established as live characters years earlier: Stanley Adams as Cyrano Jones in "...Tribbles," and Roger C. Carmel as the title character in "Mudd's..." Other guest voices of interest were those of Mark Leonard reprising his role as Spock's father, Sarek ("Yesteryear"), and Ted Knight (of Mary Tyler Moore fame) as the shape-shifting Vendorian, Carter Winston ("The Survivor").

Although occasionally hampered by Filmation's traditional stock footage/musical score "re-use" method of cost-cutting, the animated series holds up as an entertaining companion to its live-action relatives in that the scripts were appealing to both old and young alike. Prominent sci-fi author, Larry Niven, wrote "The Slaver Weapon,". Alan Dean Foster in his Star Trek Log series spanning ten volumes novelized all of the episodes. In that Foster had never actually seen the animated series and thus based his loose adaptations on the scripts he had read, the Logbooks harbor many inconsistencies in comparison to the series itself. Although the animated show won an Emmy award("Yesteryear") in 1975 for Best Children's Series, it was cancelled at the close of its two-year commitment...but not without first having earned a respectable place in ongoing Star Trek lineage.

STAR TREK
- [ ] YESTERYEAR
- [ ] ONE OF OUR PLANETS IS MISSING
- [ ] THE LORELEI SIGNAL
- [ ] MORE TROUBLES WITH TRIBBLES
- [ ] THE SURVIVOR
- [ ] THE INFINITE VULCAN
- [ ] THE MAGICKS OF MEGAS-TU
- [ ] MUDD'S PASSION
- [ ] THE TERRATIN INCIDENT
- [ ] THE TRAP
- [ ] THE AMBERGRIS ELEMENT
- [ ] SLAVER WEAPON
- [ ] BEYOND THE FARTHEST STAR
- [ ] THE EYE OF THE BEHOLDER
- [ ] THE JIHAD

SECOND SEASON
- [ ] THE PIRATES OF ORION
- [ ] BEM
- [ ] PRACTICAL JOKER
- [ ] ALBATROSS
- [ ] HOW SHARPER THAN A SERPENT'S TOOTH
- [ ] THE COUNTER CLOCK INCIDENT

THE NEW ADVENTURES OF SUPERMAN

Broadcast History:
THE NEW ADVENTURES OF SUPERMAN
Network Premiere: CBS, September, 1966 Saturday Morning

THE SUPERMAN / AQUAMAN HOUR OF ADVENTURE
Network Premiere: CBS, September, 1967 Saturday Morning

THE BATMAN / SUPERMAN HOUR
Network Premiere: CBS, September, 1968 Saturday Morning

Syndication Premiere:
SUPERMAN / BATMAN / AQUAMAN
Fall, 1977

Executive Producer: Allen Ducovny
Producers: Lou Scheimer, Norm Prescott
Director: Hal Sutherland
Story Editor: Mort Weisinger
Art Director: Don Christensen

Principal Characters and Voices:
SUPERMAN / CLARK KENT .... Collyer
LOIS LANE...........................…....................…......Joan Alexander
JIMMY OLSEN ....…......Jack Grimes
SUPERBOY / YOUNG CLARK KENT ….........Bob Hastings
LANA LANE ……………….........................Janet Waldo
SUPERMAN NARRATOR..................................Jackson Beck
SUPERBOY NARRATOR......….....................……....Ted Knight

Filmation Associates was formed in 1963 by radio announcer Norm Prescott, former Bozo the Clown animator Lou Scheimer, and former Disney animator Hal Sutherland. The fledgling outfit saw the opportunity of a lifetime in the possible chance to secure a major network deal to animate a major comic book company's lead character three years later. But how to instill to National Periodical Publications the confidence that their tiny operation could be trusted with "superhero number one?" Well, National (now known as DC Comics), decided to inspect the little storefront and check them out for themselves.

Knowing that they were soon to arrive, Scheimer proceeded to put all of his relatives, friends, etc. in "working positions" at the studio. When the National execs made their appearance, to really impress them, Scheimer, while guiding them around the studio "caught" one of his "employees" in a "minor infraction" and summarily (and loudly) "fired" him. The display of Scheimer's "tough-mindedness" convinced National execs that, indeed, Superman was in the right hands and work commenced soon afterwards.

The New Adventures of Superman with the Superman comic book's Mort Weisinger serving as the series' story editor, and Superman comic book writers George Kashdan, Bob Haney, and Leo Dorfman scripting many of the episodes, were a very faithful adaptation to the comic book mythos. They began with the title sequence, which retold the "Faster than a speeding bullet..." legend previously established in the character's media adaptations (the 40's radio show and Fleischer animated shorts, the late 40's movie serials, and the 50's live-action television series). In addition, several of the voices from the 40's radio show, including "Superman/Clark Kent" Clayton "Bud" Collyer, "Lois Lane" Joan Alexander, and narrator Jackson Beck reprised their roles for the new cartoons.

The half-hour format consisted of two six-minute Superman stories in which he and the familiar cast of characters (reporter Lois Lane, cub reporter Jimmy Olsen, and Daily Planet editor Perry White) were placed into constant jeopardy by the various denizens of Superman's Rogue's gallery. Among them were Superman's boyhood friend, now current arch-enemy and criminal scientist Lex Luthor, the alien robot Brainiac, the genius

SUPERMAN

CLARK KENT

inventor Toyman, the Prankster, puckish master of practical jokes, and the mischievous magical imp Mr. Mxyzptlk (miz-yez-pit-el-ik) from the fifth dimension land of Zriff.

Each Superman story bracketed a six-minute Superboy adventure, centering on the Man of Steel's younger days as Smallville's "Boy of Steel." The young hero teamed up with his Krypton-born pet, Krypto the Superdog, to battle an assortment of natural disasters (earthquakes, floods, hurricanes, fires), alien invaders, and, from time to time, the occasional superhuman menace that threatened Smallville and its citizens.

Eighteen half-hours were produced in the first season. Eight more were produced in the second season when the series scored the highest shares in Saturday morning history. The next season, Superman was combined with the new Aquaman half hour to form *The Superman/Aquaman Hour of Adventure*. The following season saw eight more half-hours produced as Superman was teamed with Batman to create *The Batman/Superman Hour*. These last eight marked two stylistic changes in Filmation's Superman: the stock system of re-use animation used in the first two seasons was junked in favor of new stock animation that hewed closer to main Superman artist Curt Swan's designs, and the Superman tales became two-parters in the style of the two-part Batman stories also running in the series.

Filmation's final use of the character appeared as a guest appearance in its 1972 animated *Brady Kids*' series. In "Cindy's Super Friend" the hero (with the voice of Keith Sutherland) encountered his arch-weakness Kryptonite in an unusual place... Bobby Brady's rock collection. This guest appearance launched Superman into a thirteen-year membership in Hanna-Barbera's *Super Friends* the following year.

SUPERMAN
- ☐ THE CHIMP WHO MADE IT BIG
- ☐ THE IMP-PRACTICAL JOKER
- ☐ LUTHOR STRIKES AGAIN
- ☐ THE DEADLY DISH
- ☐ THE LAVA MEN
- ☐ THE IRON EATER
- ☐ WAR OF THE BEE BATTALION
- ☐ RETURN OF BRAINIAC
- ☐ THE FORCE PHANTOM
- ☐ SUPERMAN MEETS BRAINIAC
- ☐ THE MERMEN OF EMOR
- ☐ THE MALEVOLENT MUMMY
- ☐ SEEDS OF DISASTER
- ☐ THE DEADLY ICEBERGS
- ☐ MAGNETIC MONSTER
- ☐ FIRE PHANTOM
- ☐ HALYAH OF THE HIMALAYAS
- ☐ A.P.E. STRIKES AGAIN

- BIRD MEN FROM LOST VALLEY
- SUPERMAN'S DOUBLE TROUBLE
- LUTHOR'S FATAL FIREWORKS
- TWO FACES OF SUPERMAN
- MERLIN'S MAGIC MARBLES
- THE INVISIBLE RAIDERS
- MISSION TO PLANET PERIL
- NEOLITHIC NIGHTMARE
- THE PERNICIOUS PARASITE
- THE TOYS OF DOOM
- ROBOT OF RIGA
- APE ARMY OF THE AMAZON
- THE ATOMIC SUPERMAN
- DEADLY SUPER-DOLL
- MEN FROM A.P.E.
- THE TOYMAN'S SUPER-TOY
- CAGE OF GLASS
- NIGHT OF THE OCTOPOD
- LUMINIANS ON THE LOOSE (PART I - II)
- THE GHOST OF KILBANE CASTLE (PART I - II)
- THE JAPANESE SANDMAN (PART I - II)
- THE MYSTERIOUS MR. MIST
- RAIN OF IRON (PART I - II)
- TEAM OF TERROR (PART I - II)
- LUTHOR'S LETHAL LASER (PART I - II)
- CAN A LUTHOR CHANGE HIS SPOTS? (PART I - II)

SUPERBOY
- THE TERRIBLE TRIO
- SUPER CLOWN OF SMALLVILLE
- A DEVIL OF A TIME
- SUPERBOY'S SUPER-DILEMMA
- KRYPTO, SUPER SEEING EYE DOG
- SUPERBOY MEETS MIGHTY LAD
- DOUBLE TROUBLE, DOUBLE DOOM
- DEEP SEA DRAGON
- THE MAN WHO KNEW SUPERBOY'S SECRET
- OPERATION COUNTER INVASION
- VISITOR FROM THE EARTH'S CORE
- SUPERBOY'S STRANGEST FOE
- THE BEAST THAT WENT BERSERK
- THE JINXED CIRCUS
- THE NEANDERTHAL CAVEMAN CAPER
- KRYPTO'S CAPRICIOUS CRONY
- THE SPACE REFUGEES

- THE MONSTER MOLECULE
- THE HURRICANE FIGHTERS
- THE FINGER OF DOOM
- KRYPTO, K-9 DETECTIVE
- ATTACK OF THE SUPER-SPACEMAN
- FORGET-ME-NOT-SUPERDOG
- KING SUPERBOY
- THE GREAT SPACE RACE

TARZAN, LORD OF THE JUNGLE AND THE SUPER 7

Broadcast History:
TARZAN, LORD OF THE JUNGLE

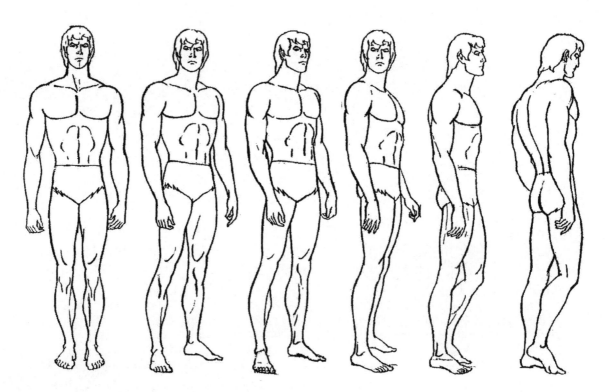

Network Premiere: CBS, September, 1976, Saturday Mornings

THE BATMAN / TARZAN ADVENTURE HOUR
Network Premiere: CBS, September, 1977, Saturday Mornings

TARZAN AND THE SUPER 7
Network Premiere: CBS, September, 1978, Saturday Mornings

THE TARZAN / LONE RANGER ADVENTURE HOUR
Network Premiere: CBS, September, 1980, Saturday Mornings

THE TARZAN / LONE RANGER / ZORRO ADVENTURE HOUR
NetworkPremiere: CBS, September, 1981, Saturday Mornings

Principal Characters and Voices:
TARZAN...Robert Ridgely
N'KIMA (Tarzan's monkey) .... Lou Scheimer

WEB WOMAN / KELLY WEBSTER .... Linda Gary
SPINNER (Web Woman's pet) .... Lou Scheimer

MANTA .... Joe Stern
MORAY .... Joan Van Ark

SUPERSTRETCH / CHRIS CROSS …............... Ty Henderson
MICROWOMAN / CHRISTY CROSS ……..........Kim Hamilton

ISIS ....Diane Pershing
HERCULES ....Bob Denison
SUPER SAMURAI / MERLIN / SINBA................Michael Bell

Tarzan, Lord of the Jungle, swung into fantastic civilizations in his first animated series. Orphaned as a child when his parents died in Africa, the animated Tarzan was raised by a she-ape named Kala, who taught him the ways of the jungle. Partnered with Nikima, a spider monkey, the apeman shared the trust and friendship of all the jungle animals. He summoned his creatures with an oscillating call and used his cunning and strength to protect the jungle and others that would come to the jungle. Tarzan's exploits happened in lost cities and hidden empires where he championed the cause of justice and good versus evil and oppression.

Tarzan was not only the beginning of another long-running addition to the Filmation stable, but it signified several major changes in the stylistic approach Filmation took to its adventure animation. Gone were the childish dots-for-eyes and the simplified approach to its adventure characters begun with The New Adventures of Superman and continued through Star Trek. In its place were both a more detailed and realistic approach to anatomy and a more defined look to the character, based partly on Tarzan artist Burne Hogarth's renditions. There was a greater reliance on body rotoscope animation and Filmation's use of "reuse" animation, known as their "stock system." The use of stock was refined to such an extent that an entire all-new episode of Tarzan produced in 1978 was done without animating a single scene of new footage…it was all done with existing stock animation.

❑ **animation by** FILMATION

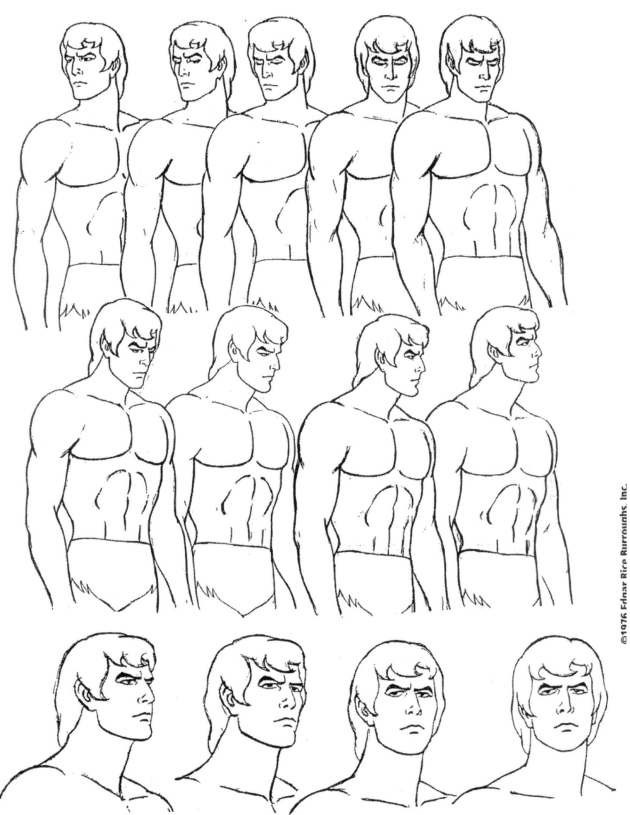

the 1978-79 season, Tarzan, Lord of the Jungle became Tarzan and the Super 7 in a ninety-minute package. Eight new Tarzan episodes and reruns were the lead-in to some new components including: Kelly Webster, who was endowed with the power of all insects throughout the galaxy as Web Woman; she was guided by Scarab, her mentor from a strange and distant planet; and she was assisted by her little furry partner, Spinner. Web Woman fought evil in many forms. A pair of water titans, Manta and Moray, Monarchs of the Deep, fought evil on and under the seven seas. The aquatic stars swam forth to keep the freedom of the seas in tropic and arctic waters alike. Superstretch and Microwoman were married couple Chris and Christy Cross. Chris could stretch his elastic form to any shape he desired, and Christy could shrink herself down to any size she needed. With the help of their dog, Trouble, they would battle evil whenever they were needed. From the Valley of Time, home of the Freedom Force, came: Merlin, master of magic; Sinbad, hero of the seven seas; Super Samurai, the young boy Toshi who, whenever he called out the name Super Samurai, became a giant of justice; mounted astride his flying horse, Pegasus, was the earth's strongest man, Hercules; and the leader of the group, the superheroine Isis, goddess of the elements. This mighty team used its powers singly or in combination in fantasy adventures to battle evil throughout its valley.

Along with the other segments of Tarzan and the Super 7 was a live-action Sci-Fi adventure series, Jason of Star Command, a spin-off of the previous season's Space Academy.

Later, The New Adventures of The Lone Ranger and The New Adventures of Zorro joined the series as part of the Tarzan, Lone Ranger, Zorro Adventure Hour.

TARZAN, LORD OF THE JUNGLE
- ☐ TARZAN AND THE CITY OF GOLD
- ☐ TARZAN AND THE VIKINGS
- ☐ TARZAN AND THE GOLDEN LION
- ☐ TARZAN AND THE FORBIDDEN CITY
- ☐ TARZAN AND THE GRAVEYARD OF THE ELEPHANTS
- ☐ TARZAN'S RETURN TO THE CITY OF GOLD
- ☐ TARZAN AND THE STRANGE VISITORS
- ☐ TARZAN AND THE LAND OF THE GIANTS
- ☐ TARZAN AND THE KNIGHTS OF NIMMR
- ☐ TARZAN'S RIVAL
- ☐ TARZAN IN THE CITY OF SORCERY
- ☐ TARZAN AT THE EARTH'S CORE
- ☐ TARZAN AND THE ICE MONSTER
- ☐ TARZAN AND THE OLYMPIAD
- ☐ TARZAN'S TRIAL
- ☐ TARZAN THE HATED
- ☐ TARZAN AND THE BIRD PEOPLE
- ☐ TARZAN AND THE SUNKEN CITY OF ATLANTIS
- ☐ TARZAN AND THE COLOSSUS OF ZOM
- ☐ TARZAN AND THE BEAST IN THE IRON MASK
- ☐ TARZAN AND THE AMAZON PRINCESS
- ☐ TARZAN AND THE CONQUISTADORS
- ☐ TARZAN AND THE SPIDER PEOPLE
- ☐ TARZAN AND THE SPACE GOD
- ☐ TARZAN AND THE LOST WORLD
- ☐ TARZAN AND THE MONKEY GOD
- ☐ TARZAN AND THE HAUNTED FOREST
- ☐ TARZAN AND THE ISLAND OF DR. MORPHOS
- ☐ TARZAN AND THE SIFU
- ☐ TARZAN AND JANE
- ☐ TARZAN AND THE LAND BENEATH THE EARTH
- ☐ TARZAN AND THE DROUGHT
- ☐ TARZAN AND THE SOUL STEALER
- ☐ TARZAN AND THE FUTURE KING
- ☐ TARZAN AND THE HUNTRESS
- ☐ TARZAN AND THE WHITE ELEPHANT

MANTA AND MORAY
- ☐ THE WATERS OF DOOM
- ☐ THE WHALE KILLERS
- ☐ THE WARMAKERS
- ☐ SEA OF MADNESS
- ☐ THE SOUVENIR HUNTERS
- ☐ THE FREEDOM FIGHTERS
- ☐ THE SUNKEN WORLD

WEB WOMAN
- ☐ THE RAIN MAKER
- ☐ THE EYE OF THE FLY
- ☐ THE WORLD WITHIN
- ☐ MADAME MACABRE'S CALAMITY CIRCUS
- ☐ RED SAILS IN THE SUNSET
- ☐ SEND IN THE CLONES
- ☐ THE SUN THIEF
- ☐ DR. DESPAIR AND THE MOOD MACHINE
- ☐ THE PERFECT CRIME
- ☐ THE LADY IN THE LAMP

THE FREEDOM FORCE
- ☐ THE DRAGON RIDERS
- ☐ THE SCARLET SAMURAI
- ☐ THE PLANT SOLDIERS
- ☐ PEGASUS' ODYSSEY

☐ THE ROBOT

SUPERSTRETCH AND MICRO WOMAN
☐ BAD THINGS COME IN SMALL PACKAGES
☐ THE RINGMASTER
☐ THE TOYMAKER
☐ FUTURE TENSE
☐ PHANTOM OF THE SEWERS
☐ SHADOW OF THE SWAMP
☐ THE GREAT CANDY BAR CAPER
☐ THE SUPERSTRETCH BOWL
☐ SUPERSTARCH AND
☐ MAGNAWOMAN
☐ SUGAR SPICE
☐ GNOME MAN'S LAND

THE NEW ADVENTURES OF TOM AND JERRY

Broadcast History:
Network Premiere: CBS, September, 1980 Saturday Morning

Syndication:
Integrated into the **MGM TOM AND JERRY CARTOONS** syndication package with other studio's production, 1986

Producers: Norm Prescott, Lou Scheimer
Creative Director: Don Christensen

Principal Characters and Voices:
DROOPY / SLICK WOLF / SPIKE / TYKE / TOM'S OWNER- Frank Welker (first six episodes), Lou Scheimer (last ten episodes)

After Hanna-Barbera's moderately successful attempt at adapting the stars of the violence-oriented *Tom and Jerry* cartoons to the more restrictive Saturday morning arena in 1985 for ABC, MGM decided to give Hanna-Barbera's archival Filmation a shot at producing a new animated series featuring the classic duo (this move was definitely seen as "rejection" of Hanna Barbera's treatment of the characters that Bill Hannah and Joe Barbara had co-developed). One of Hannah-Barbera's and ABC's decisions on dealing with the violent altercations between the cat and mouse was to eliminate them completely, thus making the longtime adversaries comrades-in-arms. The Filmation version put them back into the familiar pursuer/pursuee roles and did as much cat-and-mouse chasing as CBS censors and Filmation's adherence to their stock system approach to animation would allow. Another obstacle in production was the scripts, often written by writers who were not used to writing six-minute chase cartoons with limited dialogue. Many times Filmation's storyboard artists would literally re-write scripts in the boarding process, punching them up with gags which eventually earned the artists co-writer credits on most of the episodes. With the additional removal of the stock Hannah-Barbara "animal tie" they gave Jerry, the tieless, tireless duo starred in two seven-minute cartoons. In each half-hour these were integrated with new *Droopy* episodes. The middle of these episodes detailed the drawling dog's dealings with his perennial enemy, the wolf (one of the board's artists, as an in-house gag, gave the wolf the name "Slick." CBS liked it and it stuck).

One unique obstacle Filmation's *Tom and Jerry* series had encountered during production in 1980 was one not usually dealt with by animation producers: the 1980 Screen Actors Guild strike. This strike's direct ramification to Filmation was the removal of SAG actor and voiceman Frank Welker from his vocal duties as Droopy for the duration of the strike (the Tom and Jerry segments, having no talking characters except for Tom's owner, were minimally affected by this development). The solution: having a producer whom could also do voices. Lou Scheimer stepped behind the mike to voice all of Welker's characters… he even provided the voice of the announcer at the end of the series' opening titles.

TOM AND JERRY
- ☐ SAY WHAT?
- ☐ NEW MOUSE IN TOWN
- ☐ MOUSE OVER MIAMI
- ☐ INVASION OF THE MOUSE SNATCHERS
- ☐ SUPERSTOCKER
- ☐ HEAVY BOOKING
- ☐ FAREWELL, SWEET MOUSE
- ☐ PILE IN THE SKY
- ☐ CAT IN THE FIDDLE
- ☐ THE PLAID BARON STRIKES AGAIN
- ☐ THE PUPPY SITTER
- ☐ THE INCREDIBLE SHRINKING CAT
- ☐ SCHOOL FOR CATS
- ☐ GET A LONG JERRY
- ☐ A CONNECTICUT MOUSE IN KING ARTHUR'S COURT
- ☐ WHEN THE ROOSTER CROWS
- ☐ SAVE THAT MOUSE
- ☐ MOST WANTED CAT
- ☐ PIED PIPER PUSS
- ☐ JERRY'S COUNTRY COUSIN
- ☐ MECHANICAL FAILURE
- ☐ KITTY HAWK KITTY
- ☐ SPIKE'S BIRTHDAY
- ☐ UNDER THE BIG TOP
- ☐ SNOW BRAWL
- ☐ THE GREAT MOUSINI
- ☐ THE TROJAN DOG
- ☐ GOPHER IT, TOM
- ☐ NO MUSEUM
- ☐ STAGE STRUCK

DROOPY
- ☐ DROOPY'S RESTLESS NIGHT
- ☐ MATTERHORN DROOPY
- ☐ DISCO DROOPY
- ☐ PEST IN THE WEST
- ☐ THE INCREDIBLE DROOP
- ☐ SCARED BEAR
- ☐ STAR CROSSED WOLF
- ☐ OLD MOTHER HUBBARD
- ☐ LUMBER JERKS
- ☐ THE GREAT DIAMOND HEIST
- ☐ FOREIGN LEGION DROOPY
- ☐ GETTING A FOOT
- ☐ A DAY AT THE BAKERY
- ☐ THE GREAT TRAIN ROBBERY
- ☐ DROOPY'S GOOD LUCK CHARM

UNCLE CROC'S BLOCK

Component Series:
FRAIDY CAT, WACKY AND PACKY, and **M.U.S.H.**

Broadcast History:

Network Premiere: ABC, September 1975, Saturday Mornings

Syndicated Premiere: **THE GROOVIE GOOLIES AND FRIENDS** Fall 1977

Executive Producers: Louis Scheimer, Norman Prescott
Producer / Director Live Action: Mack Bing
Producer Animation: Don Christensen
Writers: Chuck Menville, Len Janson, Marc Richards, Mark Fink, Bill Danch, Chet Dowling

Live-Action Cast:
UNCLE CROC ....Charles Nelson Reilly
MR. RABBIT EARS ....Alife Wise
BASIL BITTERBOTTOM .... Jonathan Harris

Principal Characters and Voices:
FRAIDY CAT / TINKER / MOUSE / HONKEY .
....Alan Oppenheimer
TONKA / WIZARD / CAPTAIN KITT / SIR \
WALTER CAT / WINSTON.......... Lennie Weinrib

BULLSEYE / TROOOPER JOE / SONAR /
HILDA .... Robert Ridgel
SIDEBURNS / COLDLIPS / COLONEL FLAKE/
GENERAL UPHEAVAL........................Ken Mars

WACKY AND PACKY...................... Allan Melvin

Uncle Croc's Block, an hour-length, live action/animated series produced by Filmation for ABC in the 1975-76 season, made history for both the studio and the network in several ways (not all of them ones either party wanted).

It was the first time Filmation had ever produced a series that was a combination of both animated and live action (with the exception of the live-action intros of the animated Fat Albert and the Cosby Kids). It used live-action-programming intros to two thirds of the available Saturday morning airtime in the mid-1970's due to its costs versus the more expensive animated fare. ABC also recalled the ratings success of the similarly-formatted Hanna-Barbera's Banana Splits Adventure Hour that ran several seasons before on NBC, and felt that a similar show could serve as the lynch pin culmination of two of Filmation's ultimate goals: their major entry into what they saw as "sophisticated satire for children," and the first long-form show they produced in which they owned all of the characters and concepts featured in it.

The series had another "first" going for it: it was the first Saturday morning show to feature a thoroughly unlikable lead character: the title character, Uncle Croc, portrayed by veteran comic actor Charles Nelson Reilly, who starred in the series' live-action half. Uncle Croc served as both the host of this show as well as in the fictional Uncle Croc's Block, which accommodated Filmation's spoof of locally-produced children's shows hosted by live-action actors (e.g. Bozo the Clown). However, unlike the jolly public image generated by those hosts, the irascible Uncle Croc hated his job. This was partly due to the duties his job entailed and partly due to the ridiculous crocodile suit he wore as part of his character. His bitter attitude was also partly attributed to the callous treatment he was constantly subjected to by the show's director, the overbearing Basil Bitterbottom. This character was portrayed by Filmation veteran voiceman/actor Jonathan Harris who, like Croc, shared the same "what-am-I-doing-here?" sentiment and disdain for his occupation. These two, along with Croc's costumed funny-bunny co-host, Mr. Rabbit Ears (Alfie Wise), cavorted through comic segments that not only spoofed the live kid's show genre, but also sent up kid's heroes of all sorts. A variety of characters satirizing various stars familiar to kids (e.g. The $6.95 Man, Bogey Bear, Captain Marbles, Junie the Genie, Miss Invis, Shazowie!, Koo-Koo Keneval) made their appearances throughout the program.

Accompanying the live segments were several cartoons featuring original animated creations from Filmation that spoofed various TV genres. The venerable live-action series M.A.S.H.

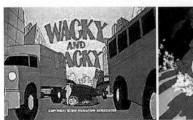

BULLSEYE
Wisecracking hound. The hero of our show.

TROOPER JOE
Bullseye's best pal. Speaks with a John Wayne accent.

COL. FLAKE
An older, slightly dingy bloodhound. He's the commander of all the other Mush dogs.

MAJOR SIDEBURNS
A finicky, whiny tattletale. He's always trying to catch Bullseye and Trooper Joe up to no good.

canine cast of characters was led by a wiseguy dog, Bullseye, and his "Trooper John"-ish partner, Trooper Joe, and was accompanied by the "Radar"-like dachshund Sonar and also by easy-going Colonel Flake. Together they strove to continually pull fast ones over the eyes of their adversaries: Cold Lips, Major Sideburns, and General Upheaval.

Other cartoon segments were "Fraidy Cat," which centered on the misadventures of the Don Knotts-ish Fraidy, a cat whose cowardice throughout the ages had already cost eight of his nine lives. He therefore lived always in fear of losing his ninth and last one. This was a bit nihilistic for a Saturday morning kid's cartoon premise, yet it was also a symbol of just how far Filmation was willing to push the envelope. Part of the gimmick as well was that he couldn't say any of the numbers "1" through "9." If he said any number between "1" and "8," one of his ghostly "predecessors" would appear, usually with the intention of unwittingly making his already tenuous situation even worse. If he had said "9" however, a stromcloud would then appear (launching lightning bolts toward the fleeing Fraidy) with intentions of divesting him of his last life. After this fun and merriment, viewers would be treated to the exploits of "Wacky and Packy," a stupid caveman and his even-stupider pet pachyderm who found themselves trapped in the present day world. Each week they sought ways to find their way home, stopping every so often to figure out ways to hustle food from the "natives."

Although ABC was extremely happy with the series (they gave it a prime Saturday AM slot), they were reportedly less than happy once they saw the first completed episodes they had commissioned. The skits seemed to fall flat timing-wise, and the general tone of cynicism reflected in the show seemed to be reflected in a reality sense as well. But the real kiss of doom was given to the show from the double barrels of the critics and ratings; it was the worst reviewed series ABC had ever aired on Saturday mornings up to that time. And worse still, it garnished some of the lowest ratings a new series had ever earned. After eight airings, ABC had the show shortened to a half-hour, dropping "Wacky and Packy" and "Fraidy Cat."

This move helped neither the critical response nor its ratings' flow. Plans were instigated to rerun Groovie Goolies in shortened form with a new title Super Fiends (a play on the title of the network's hit Super Friends series), yet the ratings by February were so bad that the series set another first for ABC: its first mid-season cancellation! It was a last for ABC as well, as the show's failure so soured ABC's opinion of Filmation that they never ordered another series from the studio again.

UNCLE CROC
- [ ] NO DOZE
- [ ] OVERWORKED AND UNDERPAID
- [ ] THE SECRET ADMIRER
- [ ] WE TRY HARDER
- [ ] A STAR IS CORN
- [ ] HAUNTED HOUSE
- [ ] YOU HAVE NO BUSINESS IN THE SHOW BUSINESS
- [ ] INFERIOR DECORATOR
- [ ] ONE OF OUR PHOTO ALBUMS IS MISSING
- [ ] THE BRAT
- [ ] O' UNLUCKY DAY
- [ ] BITTERBOTTOM'S BETTER BARGAIN
- [ ] EL CHEAPO
- [ ] THE BIG SWITCH IT'S MAGIC
- [ ] MR. NICE GUY

FRAIDY CAT
- [ ] THE NOT SO NICE MICE
- [ ] CUPID AND THE CAT
- [ ] OVER THE WALL AND HAVIN' A BALL
- [ ] FELINE FORTUNE
- [ ] PUSS "N" BOATS
- [ ] A SCAREDY FRAIDY
- [ ] MEANER THAN A JUNKYARD CAT
- [ ] FRAIDY GONE FISHIN'
- [ ] FRAIDY COME HOME
- [ ] DOUBLE TROUBLE
- [ ] LOVE IS A MANY FEATHERED THING
- [ ] IT'S A DOG'S LIFE
- [ ] UNLUCKY FRAIDY
- [ ] THIS CAT FOR HIRE
- [ ] CHOO-CHOO FRAIDY
- [ ] MAGIC NUMBERS
- [ ] A SEMI-STAR IS BORN
- [ ] CULTURE SCHLOCK

M.U.S.H.
- [ ] I AM COMMANDING OFFICER
- [ ] THE CAMP SHOW
- [ ] CAT ON A COLD TIN ROOF
- [ ] THE BIG BUDGET CUT
- [ ] THE MOOSE WHO CAME TO DINNER
- [ ] MAKE ROOM FOR CANDI
- [ ] THE CRASH DIET
- [ ] MAN CANNOT LIVE ON ICE ALONE
- [ ] HOME SWEET HAUNT
- [ ] HI-BROW MENACE
- [ ] NO TALENT SHOW
- [ ] MAJOR MYNAH
- [ ] MORE POWER TO YA
- [ ] COWERING IN THE CORNER
- [ ] THE ICEMAN MELTATH
- [ ] THE GREAT GOLD MUSH
- [ ] SIDEBURNS' SURPRISE PARTY
- [ ] THE MUSHIEST ATHLETE
- [ ] LOVE MAKES THE WORLD GO AROUND…
- [ ] WILL THE REAL SIDEBURNS PLEASE STAND UP?
- [ ] SLEEP CAN BE HAZARDOUS TO YOUR HEALTH
- [ ] I'M OK, YOU'RE NUTS
- [ ] TOYING AROUND WITH THE GENERAL
- [ ] ROOM AND BORED
- [ ] CINEMA WEIRDATE
- [ ] THE SIX ZILLION DOLLAR DOG
- [ ] GRIDIRON GRIEF
- [ ] 3-D TV
- [ ] TO FLEA OR NOT TO FLEA
- [ ] THE CALUMSO CAPER

WACKY AND PACKY
- [ ] THE NEW YORK SWEETS
- [ ] IN THE ZOO
- [ ] WACKY'S FRACTURED ROMANCE

FRAIDY CAT
A timid, slightly neurotic modern-day cat, haunted by the ghosts of his eight past lives. Whenever Fraidy mentions a number between one and eight, a ghost from one of his past lives shows up. But when Fraidy says nine, an ominous cloud appears and starts firing lightning bolts at him! Fraidy lives in fear that one day the cloud will hit its target, and he'll become the ninth ghost!

ELAFUNT
Fraidy's first ancestor, a jovial, but slow-witted cave cat. Elafunt always appears on the back of his pet dinosaur, ANT.

HEP CAT
A jive-talking jazz cat from the 1940's. One blast from his hot horn can level buildings.

BILLY THE KIT
A rambunctious little cowboy cat. He packs a mean pop-gun.

- [ ] PACKY COME HOME
- [ ] LET'S MAKE A BUNDLE
- [ ] ALL IN A DAY'S WORK
- [ ] THE PARTY CRUSHERS
- [ ] MAGIC MAYHEM
- [ ] THE BAD NEWS CRUISE

- ☐ THE FENDER BENDERS
- ☐ UNCLE SAM WANTS YOU?
- ☐ NO PLACE LIKE HOME
- ☐ ONE OF OUR MISSING LINKS IS MISSING
- ☐ THE SHOPPING SPREE
- ☐ GETTING A PIECE OF THE ROCK
- ☐ IS THIS ANY WAY TO RUN AN AIRLINE?

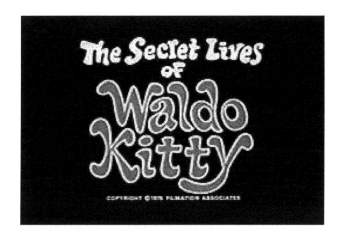

THE NEW ADVENTURES OF WALDO KITTY
(*also known as* **THE SECRET LIVES OF WALDO KITTY**)

Broadcast History:
Network Premiere: NBC, September, 1975 Saturday Mornings

Syndication Premiere:
THE GROOVIE GOOLIES AND FRIENDS
Fall, 1979

Executive Producers: Norm Prescott, Lou Scheimer
Creative Director: Don Christenson
Writers: Jim Ryan, Bill Danch

Principal Characters And Voices:
WALDO / CATMAN / CATZAN / LONE KITTY / ROBIN CAT / CAPTAIN HERC……….....………………Howard Morris
FELICIA / SPARROW / LT. O-HOO-HA………........Jane Webb
TYRONE / MR. CROC / DR. MOANS…………Allan Melvin

With the advent of the 1975 season, Filmation entered two areas they had only dabbled in previously. For the first time, its production out represented more Filmation-created characters than other companies' licensed creations. Also, Filmation decided to extend their typical "animated sitcom" focus and reach into the realm of satire as a focus for their comedy. One of Filmation's layout artists, Lorna Smith, a rabid cat-fancier, submitted an idea to the studio for an animated version of the James Thurber classic, The Secret Lives of Walter Mitty, which dealt with a mild-mannered man's hidden extravagant fantasies…only done with cats.

NBC went for the concept, The Secret Lives of Waldo Kitty to which Filmation, expanding on its growing expertise and confidence in live-action production, went a step further: instead of an all-animated concept about a cat and his fantasies, they formatted the series as animated stories with live-action wraparounds featuring the cat Waldo Kitty and his kitten girlfriend, Felicia, and their encounters with the "evil" neighbor-dog, Tyrone, with voiceovers playing over the live-action. After a confrontation that usually left him on the losing end, our hero would then fantasize about what he would do if he was, rather than the meek Waldo, his favorite hero instead.

The live-action then dissolved into animation as the show would segue into comedy "tails" that were satirical spoofs of various live-action concepts that, ironically, Filmation had either before or would in their future produce straight animated adventures of Catzan (Tarzan), Catman and Sparrow (Batman and Robin), The Lone Kitty (The Lone Ranger), Robin Cat (Robin Hood), and Cat Trek (Star Trek). Originally planned to feature three episodes of each concept during the series run, the reduction of NBC episode orders from the previous season's 16 to 13 segments that season meant that only the first three concepts mentioned had three episodes; the latter two only had two adventures produced.

One of the basic rules of satirizing an established concept is that courts have ruled in various cases it is all right to do occasional spoofs as long as an entire series is not built solely on the same concept…at least without permission of the original concept's owner. For this reason, the James Thurber estate instituted legal proceedings against the studio for infringing on its copyrights re: Walter Mitty/Waldo Kitty. As a result, when the series finished its season-long run on NBC and went into syndication later as part of *The Groovie Goolies* package of several Filmation series and was retitled *The New Adventures of Waldo Kitty*, the concept of the live-action kitty dreaming of "fantasies" dropped with the removal of the live wraparounds. Dropping the two minutes of wraps also helped adjust the episode's running time; since syndication allowed more time for commercial space than network programs, the 21-minute adjusted episode time allowed for the insertion of more commercials per episode without losing any story.

Another legal problem with the series was narrowly averted when the studio settled (shortly before airing the series) with Lorna Smith, who threatened to sue when she felt the studio was not going to give her the proper credit for the series idea. Filmation refused at first, since she was already an employee of the studio, but later compromised and settled on a rare "based on an idea by Lorna Smith" credit for the show. Considering the legal troubles they later fell into, one wonders sometimes if they would have been better off just forgetting the whole thing.

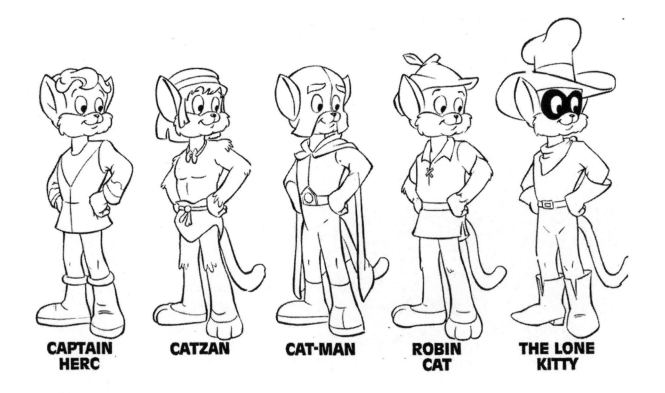

THE NEW ADVENTURES OF WALDO KITTY
- [ ] CAT MAN
- [ ] CATZAN OF THE APES
- [ ] THE LONE KITTY
- [ ] ROBIN CAT
- [ ] CAT TREK
- [ ] CAT MAN MEETS THE POOCHQUIN
- [ ] CATZAN OR NOT CATZAN
- [ ] THE LONE KITTY RIDES AGAIN
- [ ] SHERIFF OF SHERWOOD
- [ ] CAT MAN MEETS THE PUZZLER
- [ ] DR. LIVINGSTONE, I PERFUME?
- [ ] PING OF PONGO
- [ ] CHAW THE BULLET

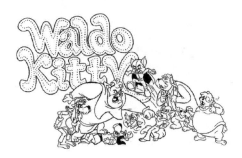

WILL THE REAL JERRY LEWIS, PLEASE SIT DOWN?

Broadcast History:
Network Premiere: ABC September, 1970 Saturday Morning

Executive Producers: Norm Prescott, Lou Scheimer
Director: Hal Sutherland
Writers: Bill Danch, Bill Ryan, Len Janson, Chuck Menville and Jack Mendelsohn

Principal Characters and Voices:
JERRY LEWIS ....David L. Lander

JERRALDINE LEWIS / RHONDA ....Jane Webb
MR. BLUNDERBUSS / RALPH ROTTEN LEWIS / WON TON SON / PROFESSOR LEWIS / HONG KONG LEWIS / UNCLE SEADOG ....Howard Morris

The ABC network's half-hour series Will the Real Jerry Lewis Please Sit Down? caricatured the multi-talented, movie star comic for a cartoon series based on his live-action film *The Family Jewels*. All supporting guest cast members were designed to look like characters based in the movie, and Jerry himself played many of these roles. In this animated series, Jerry Lewis worked for the Odd Job Employment Agency, which was owned by the pompous and bullying Mr. Blunderbuss. As a last substitute choice, he was assigned a variety of temporary assignments in which he always caused some sort of mishap. The regular supporting characters were: his absent-minded, nutty professor father; his kid-sister, Jerraldine; his girlfriend, Rhonda; and his pet frog, Spot.

Lewis did not voice his animated character in the series (David L. Lander, "Squiggy" on TV's *Laverne and Shirley*, provided the voice characterization), but did contribute to several stories.

WILL THE REAL JERRY LEWIS, PLEASE SIT DOWN ?
☐ JERRY HORNS IN
☐ COMPUTER SUITOR
☐ MOVIE MADNESS
☐ CRASH COURSE
☐ JERRY GOES APE
☐ TWO-AND-A-HALF RING CIRCUS
☐ HAUNTED HOUSE GUEST
☐ GOOD LUCK CHARM
☐ BUTLER'S PENTHOUSE
☐ OUT TO LAUNCH
☐ SHIPBOARD ROMANCE
☐ WATCH ON THE RHINO
☐ HOCUS POCUS
☐ HOW GREEN WAS MY VALET
☐ DOUBLE TROUBLE
☐ RAINMAKER
☐ DOUBLE OH OH

animation by FILMATION

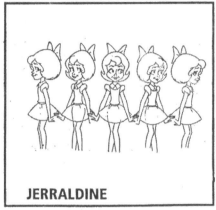

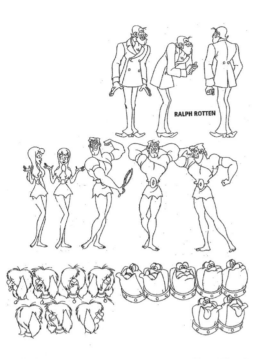

THE NEW ADVENTURES OF ZORRO

Broadcast History:
THE TARZAN / LONE RANGER / ZORRO ADVENTURE HOUR
Network Premiere: CBS September, 1981 Saturday Morning

Executive Producers: Norm Prescott, Lou Scheimer
Producer: Don Christensen
Story Editor: Arthur C. Brown
Writers: Arthur Brownw Jr., Marty Warner, Robby London

Principal Characters and Voices:
ZORRO / DON DIEGO ....Henry Darrow
AMIGO / MIGUEL..............…........................…….Julio Medina
CAPTAIN RAMON ....…......Eric Mason
SGT. GONZALES…..…….......................……..…...Don Diamond
MARIA........……..………...............................…...Christine Avila
LUCIA...............…………..Socorro Valdez
GASPAR...East Carlo
DON ALEJANDRO / GOV. GENERAL....…..........Carlos Rivas

The *New Adventures of Zorro*, joined the *Tarzan/Lone Ranger Adventure Hour* in 1981, once again breaking significant ground in the Filmation production cannon. For starters, the series, which centered on the adventures of the swashbuckling masked swordsman who battled the corrupt Spanish forces that ruled early California toward the end of the 1800's, was one of only two in the history of Saturday morning cartoons, (1984's *Rubik, the Amazing Cube* being the other) that featured a totally Hispanic cast of characters and actors (*Zorro*, for example, was played by Henry Darrow, who later played the fop-turned-avenger in Disney's live-action *Zorro and Son* sitcom and still later played Zorro's father in New World's live-action syndicated *Zorro* series). During its minute tags, Zorro taught the audience the Spanish words as well as the proper use of Spanish phrases.

Another significant point in the series was its constant use of swordplay between the heroes and villains. Such swordplay, along with the type of gunplay apparent in Zorro's counterpart, *The Lone Ranger*, had been previously labeled as a "kid imitatable" act by CBS's Standards and Practices Division. It turned out that one of CBS's Saturday morning programming staffers was a member of the 1976 American fencing team in that year's Olympics. Naturally, this series particularly touched his heart (no pun intended). He heartily supported the CBS buying of the series and later went on to ensure the accuracy of Zorro's swordfighting scenes by personally serving as the rotoscope model for the footage from which the stock animation was created.

The most significant groundbreaker of all though, happened in this series and was in a sense responsible for Filmation's downfall. That season, 1981, was at that time the most productive in Filmation's history. They had seven series on the air that year: *Zorro, Tarzan, The Lone Ranger, Fat Albert and the Cosby Kids, Blackstar, Shazam!,* and *Hero High* (all seven being far too much to handle domestically... as was Lou Scheimer's policy at the time). It was also during this season that all of the major studios were sending animation to subcontracting houses in Australia and Korea in an attempt to reduce production costs. Lou had considered doing this as well, however several young storyboard artists and directors on his staff convinced Lou to

send one of his series overseas to one of the top Japanese animation studios, Tokyo Movie Shinsha (*Space Cobra, Lupin III*) in order to facilitate production.

After viewing some of their product, Lou decided that these were the right people to meet his job-quality demands. He sent his most difficult series, *Zorro*, over to TMS to be produced. Despite some production hassles between the two studios, which upset Lou and producer/liason Don Christensen enough to resolve not to send another animated series to Japan, *Zorro* not only now featured technically higher quality (and a total absence of the typical Filmation "stock animation re-use" system), and not only was the best looking series produced by Filmation or any other American producer since *Flash Gordon*, but it inspired other American animation producers to start using Japanese sub-contract houses to execute their animation. It also opened the door for Japanese animation houses, particularly TMS, to start directly producing animated series for Saturday morning animation. The combination of this, as well as numerous other Japanese, Taiwanese, and Korean studios being utilized by the likes of Hanna-Barbera, Marvel, and Ruby-Spears to produce volumes of animation at cheaper rates than Filmation's domestically-produced product eventually led to Filmation's closure! It was indeed ironic that the man who was determined to keep all his animation in America was eventually undone by circumstances caused by the one time he sent a series overseas.

THE NEW ADVENTURES OF ZORRO
- THREE'S A CROWD
- FLASH FLOOD
- THE BLOCKADE
- THE FRAME
- TURNABOUT
- THE TYRANT
- TERRERMOTO!
- THE TRAP
- FORT RAMON
- THE TAKEOVER
- DOUBLE TROUBLE
- THE CONSPIRACY
- THE MYSTERIOUS TRAVELER

Animation by
FILMATION

LIVE-ACTION SERIES

LIVE-ACTION BY FILMATION

For a company that made its mark in the television industry largely on the strength of animated adventure series with human characters, it was a combination of fortuitous circumstance and timing that caused the studio to do what even Hanna-Barbera could not do. That was forge a second production success in the production of live-action Saturday morning series, with production values in the majority of them comparable to their live-action prime time counter-parts.

This was due partly to CBS' assertion that, by the winter of 1973, there were just too much animation on all networks' schedules, not just theirs. All that animation was beginning to the take on a mind-numbing similarity. During a pitch for the then animated proposal of a Shazam! series. The idea was postulated: would it be possible to produce this idea, a superhero-type that the studio was previously famous for, but had not produced in five years, since the heyday of superhero shows in the late 1960's, in the usually cost-prohibitive live-action format? Part of the reason for the profusion of hour. This was usually about half that of a similar live-action half-hour, plus the perception that kids would be bored by the relative steadiness of real people as opposed to cartoon people.

Filmation's fortuitous circumstance was in its working relationship with Robert F. Chanault, a live-action producer/director who, because of his relationship with the Wrather Corporation, served as consultant on Filmation's *Lassie's Rescue Rangers* animated series. Wrather owns the rights to the Lassie character. In addiction, he produced and directed Bill Cosby's live-action wraparounds for *Fat Albert and the Cosby Kids*. Chenault devised production methods that would bring the cast of live-action production in line with Saturday morning animation costs. Among them the extensive use of outdoor shooting. After being made Filmation's first executive producer other than Norm Prescott and Lou Scheimer, put those practices into play with the *Shazam!* series. The result was the highest rated Saturday morning series on all three networks, and a resurgence in live-action production at all three networks. *The Shazam!* success led to an equally successful spin-off *The Secret of Isis*, and several other live-action series for CBS. Although the series they did for another network, ABC's *Uncle Croc's Block* was among their biggest failures. In addition, with increasing budgets and the success of *Star Wars*, the studio was able to create a special effects and miniatures department that was the equal of most bigger-budgeted movie companies.

ARK II

Broadcast History:
Network Premiere: CBS September 1976, Saturday Mornings

Executive Producers: Norm Prescott, Lou Scheimer
Producer: Robert F. Chenault
Story Editor: Martin Roth

Starring:
Jonah	Terry Lester
Rutyh	Jean Marie-Hon
Samuel	Jose Flores
Adam	Himself
Narrator	Lou Scheimer

Filmation's fourth entry in their burgeoning and successful Saturday morning live-action production enterprise sought to combine sources as divergent as *Planet of the Apes* and The Bible into a semi-religious, sci-fi allegory. *Ark II*

also made use of Filmation's self-policing trend toward non-violent adventure (which Lou Scheimer vowed to continue in spite of what he saw as his competitors using more violence-orientated confrontations in their programs—specifically referring to ABC's *Krofft Super Show* which beat his competing *Shazam!/Isis Hour* in the ratings the season before), and use of multi-racial casts.

The premise of the series was set after a worldwide "holocaust" (hinted at possibly being caused by man) which rendered Earth barren and lifeless. This catastrophe caused man to revert back to his most primitive state. One of the few exceptions to this was a colony of scientists, hidden underneath the Earth and shielded from the holocaust, who felt that it was up to them to use their super-science to give mankind a second chance. They were three very young and quite brilliant scientists: the biblically (and appropriately) named Jonah, Ruth, and Samuel, and a super-intelligent (though mercifully non-talking) chimpanzee named Adam. The quartet emerged from the sanctuary inside their naturally named ARK II, a futuristic van housing the latest in technology and scientific equipment. Their mission: to encounter the primitive tribes that now existed, plant new agriculture, and to conduct experiments designed to set mankind back on the road to rebuilding itself. The setting of this desolate society also enabled Filmation to save money in set construction by shooting the series in the deserts outside of Los Angeles rather than building new set interiors.

ARK II
- [ ] THE FLIES
- [ ] THE RULE
- [ ] THE TANK

- ☐ THE SLAVES
- ☐ THE BALLOON
- ☐ THE MIND GROUP
- ☐ THE LOTTERY
- ☐ THE DROUGHT
- ☐ THE WILD BOY
- ☐ THE ROBOT
- ☐ OMEGA
- ☐ ROBIN HOOD
- ☐ THE CRYOGENIC MAN
- ☐ DON QUIXOTE
- ☐ ORKUS

THE GHOSTBUSTERS

Broadcast History:
Network Premiere: CBS September 1975, Saturday Mornings

Executive Producers: Norm Prescott, Lou Scheimer
Producer / Director: Arthur Nadel
Story Editor / Writer: Marc Richards

Starring:
EDDIE SPENSER .... Larry Starch
JAKE KONG .... Forrest Tucker
TRACY... Bob Burns

CBS, which took the chance of adding live-action programming to its already-successful Saturday morning slate in 1974. Filmation took the chance of branching out into live-action production. This was both encouraged by the success of their Shazam! live-action series in 1974 to produce several new live-action series the following year. Head writer Marc Richards decided to create a modern-day version of the 1940's Abbott and Costello ghost-chasing comedies.

At the time, the studio was considering casting a pair of familiar television sitcom actors in the lead rolls: the possibility of rejoining Gilligan's Island's Bob Denver and Alan Hale. With Bob Denver committed to another CBS Saturday morning series, Far Out Space Nuts, former F-Troop stars Forrest Tucker and Larry Storch were cast as mismatched Ghost Busters Spenser and Kong, with their gorilla companion Tracy portrayed by Bob Burns in a suit. To maintain the illusion for the kids, the credit read "Tracy trained by Bob Burns." The series ran for one season, later spinning off the animated version ten years later after Columbia's highly successful movie of the same name.

GHOST BUSTERS
- ☐ THE MALTESE MONKEY
- ☐ DR. WHAT'S HIS NAME
- ☐ THE CANTERVILLE GHOST
- ☐ WHO'S AFRAID OF THE BIG BAD WOLF
- ☐ THE FLYING DUTCHMAN
- ☐ THE DUMMY'S REVENGE
- ☐ THE WORTHLESS GAUZE
- ☐ WHICH WITCH IS WHICH
- ☐ THEY WENT THATAWAY
- ☐ VAMPIRE'S APPRENTICE
- ☐ JEKYLL & HYDE — TOGETHER FOR THE FIRST TIME
- ☐ ONLY GHOST HAVE WINGS
- ☐ THE VIKINGS HAVE LANDED
- ☐ MERLIN THE MAGICIAN
- ☐ THE ABOMINABLE SNOWMAN

JASON OF STAR COMMAND

Broadcast History

Tarzan and the Super 7
Network Premiere: CBS September, 1978, Saturday Mornings, 15 minute segment

Jason of Star Command
Network Premiere: CBS September, 1979, Saturday Mornings, Half-hour series

Executive Producers: Norm Prescott, Lou Scheimer
Producer: Arthur Nadel
Story Editor: Samuel Peeples

Starring:
JASON .... Craig Littler
DRAGOS .... Sid Haig
COMMANDER CANARVAN ..... James Doohan
PROFESSOR E.J. PARSAFOOT .... Charlie Dell
SAMANTHA .... Tamara Dobson
TWIKI .... Larry Storch

A spin-off from 1977's Space Academy series, Jason of Star Command was developed as a planned lower-budget version of the former series. Lower in the sense that it would only be 15 minutes per week as opposed to Space Academy's half-hour format. They envisioned capitalizing on the success the previous year of the Star Wars movie.

The series stressed action more than previous Filmation live-action series had and was structured as Saturday morning television's first serial, a la the cliffhangers of the 1940's, with a rock-ribbed hero, Jason, played by Craig Littler, who operated from the Star Command asteroid of which the Space Academy was only a part. With a hissable Darth Vader-like villain, Dragos, played by Sid Haig, who sought to conquer the galaxy, each episode ended with a cliffhanger featuring Jason and his comrades Commander Canavan, played by Star Trek's James Doohan, befuddled inventor E.J. Parsafoot, played by Charlie Dell, and his pocket-size robot companion, Twiki, whose voice was created by speeding up the soundtracks Larry Storch created for the Brady Kid's Chinese-speaking pandas, Ping and Pong.

Ironically, due to the multitude of special effects and miniatures, each fifteen minute segment cost as much as a Space Academy half-hour, and after the ratings showed that it was the highest-rated segment of the Tarzan and the Super 7, it was granted it's own half-hour series the following season. Two new characters joined the series: Jason's new supervisor, the blue-skinned Commander Stone, and the alien amazon, Tamora. Twelve half-hours were produced that season, which compared favorably to the bigger budgeted series Battlestar Galactica and Buck Rogers.

JASON OF STAR COMMAND (15 Minutes)
☐ THE GOLDEN GRYPHON STRIKES!
☐ DRAGOS - MASTER OF THE COSMOS!
☐ ESCAPE FROM DRAGOS
☐ PLUNGE TO DESTRUCTION
☐ STAR COMMAND MUST BE SAVED
☐ LIMBO OF THE LOST
☐ MAROONED IN TIME
☐ CANNONS OF LIGHT
☐ THE ADVENTURES OF PEEPO AND WICKY
☐ THE INVISIBLE MAN
☐ THE MYSTERIOUS PLANET
☐ PRISON OF LIGHT
☐ THE BLACK HOLE
☐ THE ENEMY WITHIN
☐ THE TROJAN HORSE
☐ THE FINAL ASSAULT

1979 (Half - Hour)
- ☐ BEYOND THE STARS
- ☐ SECRETS OF THE ANCIENTS
- ☐ THE POWER OF THE STAR DISK
- ☐ THROUGH THE STARGATE
- ☐ MISSION TO THE STARS
- ☐ LITTLE GIRL LOST
- ☐ FROZEN IN SPACE
- ☐ FACE TO FACE
- ☐ WEB OF THE STAR WITCH
- ☐ PHANTOM FORCE
- ☐ MIMI'S SECRET
- ☐ BATTLE FOR FREEDOM

THE SECRET OF ISIS

Broadcast History:
SHAZAM! / ISIS HOUR
Network Premiere: CBS September 1975, Saturday Mornings

Executive Producers: Norm Prescott, Lou Scheimer, Robert F. Chenault
Producer: Arthur Nadel
Writers: Sid Morse, David Wise, David and Susan Dworski, Peter and Sarah Dixon, Henry Colman, Len Janson and Chuck Menville

Starring:
ISIS / ANDREA THOMAS .... Joanna Cameron
RICK MASON .... Brain Cutler
CINDY LEE .... Joanna Pang

The Secret of Isis was one of the few Saturday morning series to star a woman in the lead role, to give young girl viewers a heroine to look up to in the same ways the boys could look up to Captain Marvel. Isis starred Joanna Cameron as school teacher Andrea Thomas who, unaware to her fellow high school teacher Rick Mason, played by Brian Cutter or her teaching assistant Cindy Lee, played by Joanna Pang, had a few secrets they knew nothing about.

Those secrets centered on the pendant that Andrea wore: an ancient Egyptian talisman she found during an archeological dig. Andrea's chanting call, "Oh mighty Isis," transforms her into the superheroic reincarnation of the Egyptian goddess of nature. As Isis, she could fly by summoning the "zephyr winds" and possessed the ability to bend all the forces of nature to her will.

From her companion series Shazam!, Billy and Mr. Mentor traveled across the country encountering kids in trouble for Captain Marvel to rescue. Andrea's high school had enough of the similarly trouble-prone youths in attendance to keep her on her toes. Occasionally, when circumstances went beyond even her control, Captain Marvel would crossover from his series to lend a superhand.

The combined Shazam!/Isis Hour was the number one rated Saturday morning series that season. Thanks to Ms. Cameron, the show featured a higher demographic percentage of adult male viewers than most primetime series.

Competing network ABC fielded its own live-action "super heroine" series the following season (1976) with the *Electro Woman and Dyna Girl* segments of their live-action *Krofft Super show*. With two elements *The Secret of Isis* series lacked, a campish faster-paced 1960's Batman tone and a kooky coterie of supervillains, *The Krofft Super show* trashed *Shazam!/Isis Hour* the following season. Filmation attributed the defeat to the former series' violent content, stating that it never put Isis into situations as perilous and irresponsible as those into which Krofft put its heroines. In 1978, Isis became an animated superheroine as part of *Tarzan and the Super 7*.

THE SECRETS OF ISIS (Half - Hour)
- ☐ LIGHTS OF MYSTERY MOUNTAIN
- ☐ SPOTS OF THE LEOPARD
- ☐ FOOL'S DARE
- ☐ THE SOUND OF SILENCE
- ☐ ROCKHOUND'S ROBOT
- ☐ LUCKY
- ☐ BIGFOOT
- ☐ TO FIND A FRIEND
- ☐ THE SHOW OFF
- ☐ THE OUTSIDER
- ☐ GIRL DRIVER
- ☐ SCUBA DUBA
- ☐ DREAMS OF FLIGHT

☐ NO DRUMS, NO TRUMPETS
☐ THE SEEING-EYE-HORSE
☐ THE HITCHHIKERS
☐ THE CHEERLEADER
☐ THE CLASS CLOWN
☐ YEAR OF THE DRAGON

(Hour Long)
☐ NOW YOU SEE IT…
☐ …AND NOW YOU DON'T (Crossover with **Shazam!**)

SHAZAM!

Broadcast History:

Network Premiere: CBS September, 1974 Saturday Mornings

Shazam! / Isis Hour
Network Premiere: CBS September 1975 Saturday Mornings

Executive Producers: Norm Prescott, Lou Scheimer
Producer: Arthur Nadel, Robert F. Chenault
Writers: Chuck Menville, Len Janson, Bill Danch, Jim Ryan, Don Glut, Sid Morse, Marc Richards, Marianne Mosner, J. Michael Reaves

Starring:
BILLY BATSON .... Michael Gray
CAPTAIN MARVEL .... Jackson Bostwick(1974 - 975), John Davey(1975 - 1977)
MENTOR .... Les Tramayne
THE ELDERS ....
.... Lou Scheimer, Norm Prescott(voices)

Filmation's first live-action Saturday morning series was partially inspired by CBS seeking to diversify the type of shows they were offering to the kids. Filmation, seeking to break out of the extremely competitive animation production pack, jockeyed for air time with such companies as Hanna-Barbera, DePatie-Freleng, and Rankin-Bass, noting the success of their new style of "programming with a message."
Filmation took a project originally developed as an animated series. Shazam! was based on DC Comics' Captain Marvel character, created by C.C. Beck and Otto Binder in 1941, and redeveloped as a live-action adventure show shot in and around the Sepulveda Basin near the studio's home base in the Los Angeles area.

The show starred teen idol Michael Gray as young Billy Batson, who traveled across the country in a motor home with his friend, Mr. Mentor, played by Les Tremayne, loosely based on the comics' actual Shazam! character. Together, they would encounter various young teens and kids with problems similar to those experienced by the show's target audiences, such as prejudice, drug use, and peer pressure.

Early in each episode, Billy would converse with the "Elders." They were so-called because the network's Standards and Practices would not allow them to be referred to as Gods—as they were in the comics. The Elders' initials formed the show's title: Soloman, Hercules, Atlas, Zeus, Achilles, and Mercury. To give them an otherworldly look, they were animated

as heavily rendered cel characters with only mouth animation.

When the situation grew too dicey for Billy and Mentor, usually demonstrated by a restatement of that episode's moral, the youth would yell the magic word "Shazam!," which would then transform him into the superhero Captain Marvel. The hero would then use his flight, super-strength, and super-speed powers to deal with the present menace. At the end of each episode Captain Marvel would again appear with that show's moral. The stories, with as much non-violent action as the censors would allow, and low-budget but well-staged stunts and special effects, were a major hit for the CBS network that season, leading the way for a variety of future live-action efforts by Filmation. This established the studio as the one production house that could produce both animation and live-action equally well.

The series ran three seasons, with John Davey replacing Jackson Bostwick as the lead character, Captain Marvel, for the last two seasons of the series after a salary dispute.

The Shazam!/Isis Hour established Captain Marvel as a spokesman for a national reading program for kids. Comic fans wanted to see their hero deal less with troubled teens and more with trouble-making villains, getting their wish several years later when Filmation produced an animated version of Captain Marvel as part of *The Kid Super Power Hour with Shazam!* for the NBC network.

SHAZAM! 1974
- THE BROTHERS
- THE LURE OF THE LOST
- THE JOYRIDERS
- THE PAST IS NOT FOREVER
- THE ROAD BACK
- THE GANG'S ALL HERE
- THE DOOM BUGGY
- THE BRAIN
- THE BOY WHO SAID "NO"
- THOU SHALT NOT KILL
- THE ATHLETE
- THE TREASURE
- LITTLE BOY LOST
- THE DELINQUENT
- THE BRAGGERT

1975
- ON WINNING
- DEBBIE
- FOOLS GOLD
- DOUBLE TROUBLE
- GOODBYE, PACKY
- SPEAK NO EVIL
- THE ODD COUPLE

1976
- THE CONTEST
- BITTER HERBS
- RIPCORD
- FINDERS KEEPERS
- THE SOUND OF A DIFFERENT DRUMMER
- OUT OF FOCUS

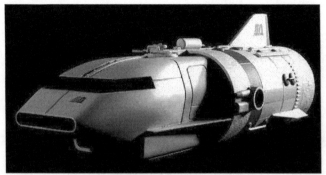

SPACE ACADEMY

Broadcast History:

Network Premiere: CBS September, 1977 Saturday Mornings

Executive Producers: Norm Prescott, Lou Scheimer
Producer / Director: Arthur Nadel
Writers: Lynn Baker, Ted Pedersen, Martha Humphreys, Samuel A. Peeples, Martin Roth, Tom Swale

Starring:
COMMANDER GOMPU	Jonathan Harris
ADRIAN	Maggie Cooper
TEE GAR	Brain Tochi
LOKI	Eric Greene
CHRIS	Ric Carrott
PEEPO	Lou Scheimer

Set in the year 3732, *Space Academy* boasted one of the largest budgets ever spent on a Saturday morning series at the time, due primarily to extensive and impressive use of special effects and miniatures, as well as scripts and concepts developed by famed sci-fi and *Star Trek* writer Samuel A. Peeples. Sci-fi genre star and veteran Filmation performer Jonathan Harris of *My Favorite Martians, Uncle Croc's Block*, and *Lost in Space*, starred as mysterious alien Commander Gampu at Space Academy. The academy was a high-tech, futuristic asteroid housing a school for the galaxy's finest young space cadets, some with telepathic, telekinetic, or other traits, as well as one of several derivations of the *Star War's* R2-D2 and C3PO androids, the ubiquitous "Peepo."

Despite the show's strong ratings that season, the high production costs forced the reconfiguration of the concept into the fifteen-minute per episode spin-off *Jason of Star Command* the following season.

SPACE ACADEMY
- [ ] THE ROCKS OF JUNE
- [ ] THERE'S NO PLACE LIKE HOME
- [ ] THE CHEAT
- [ ] MY FAVORITE MARCIA
- [ ] PLANET OF FIRE
- [ ] CASTAWAYS IN TIME AND SPACE
- [ ] THE SURVIVORS OF ZALON
- [ ] COUNTDOWN
- [ ] HIDE AND SEEK
- [ ] LIFE BEGINS AT 300
- [ ] MONKEY BUSINESS
- [ ] PHANTOM PLANET
- [ ] STAR LEGEND
- [ ] JOHNNY SUNSEED
- [ ] SPACE HOOKEY

Animation by FILMATION STORYBOARDS

STORYBOARDS BY FILMATION

Storyboarding was one of Filmation Studio's most creative and demanding production jobs. It's the one job where *the film as a whole* is planned and designed for the screen.

As a storyboard artist the demands on their time, talent and learning ability will be heavy. At times the frustrations will be high. But they were rewarded with a sense of involvement, feeling of accomplishment — and the highest production-level salary scale in the studio.

The Department was looking to train people who had four special talents: a strong sense of *design and composition*, a strong sense of *storytelling and characterization*, the ability to *learn and adapt*, and a flair for *teamwork and organization*.

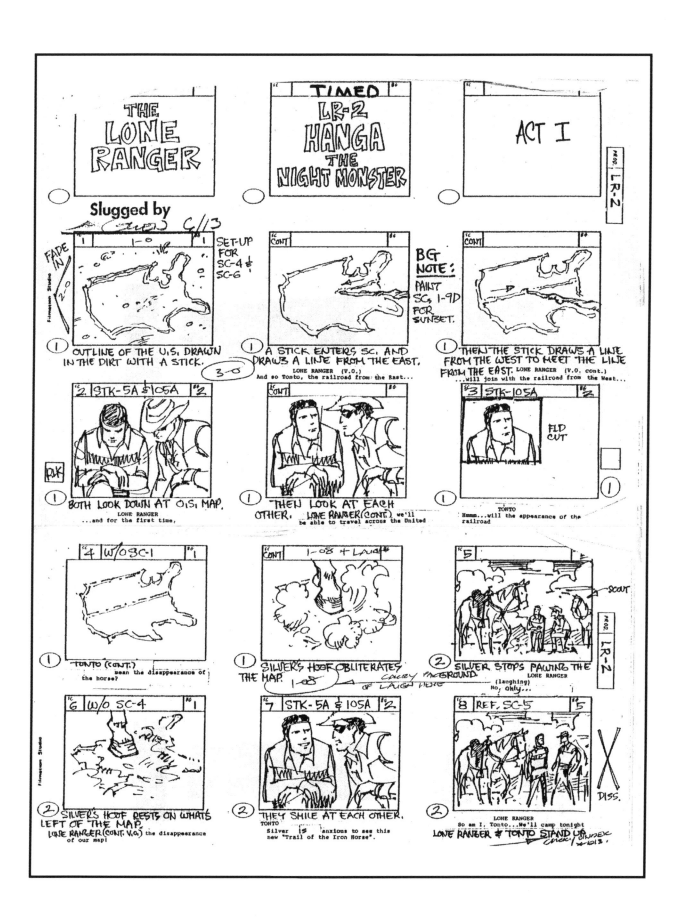

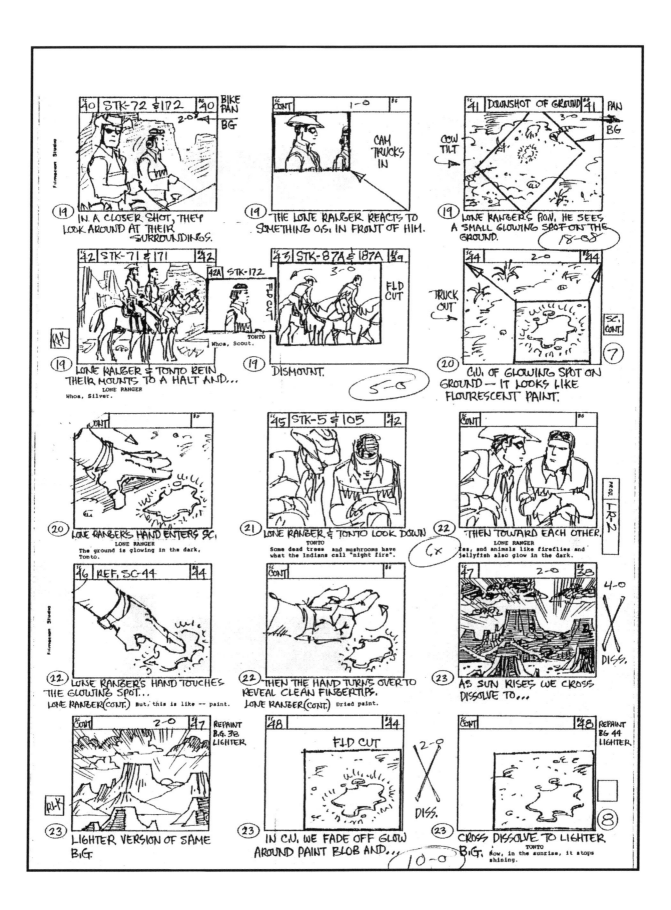

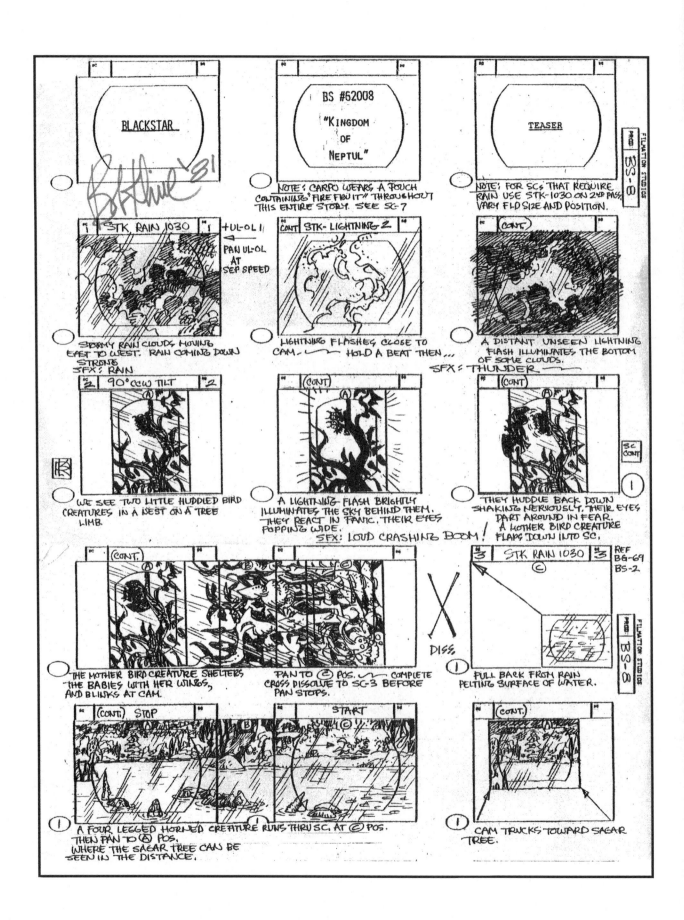

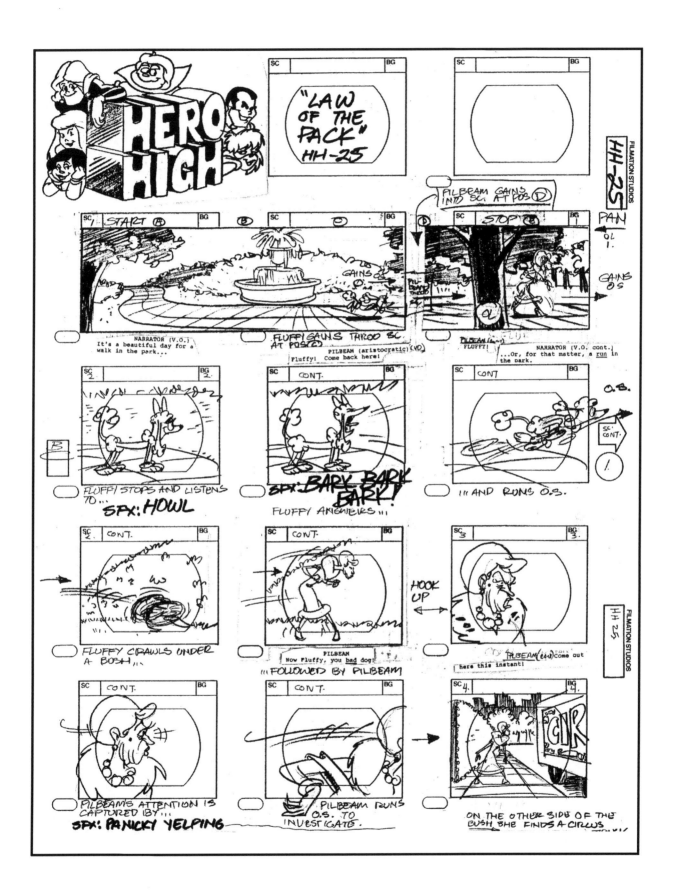

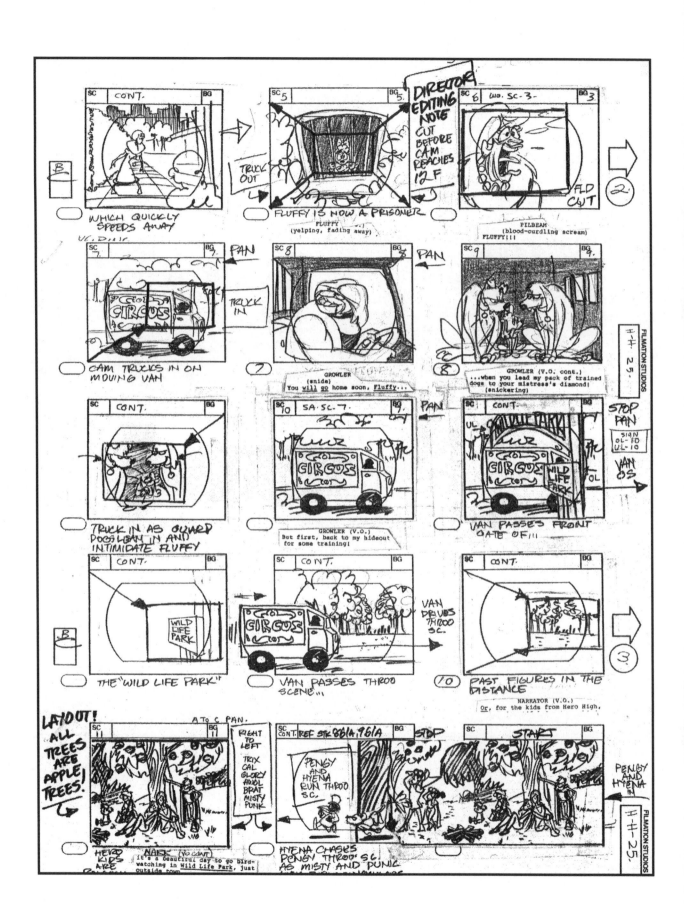

161

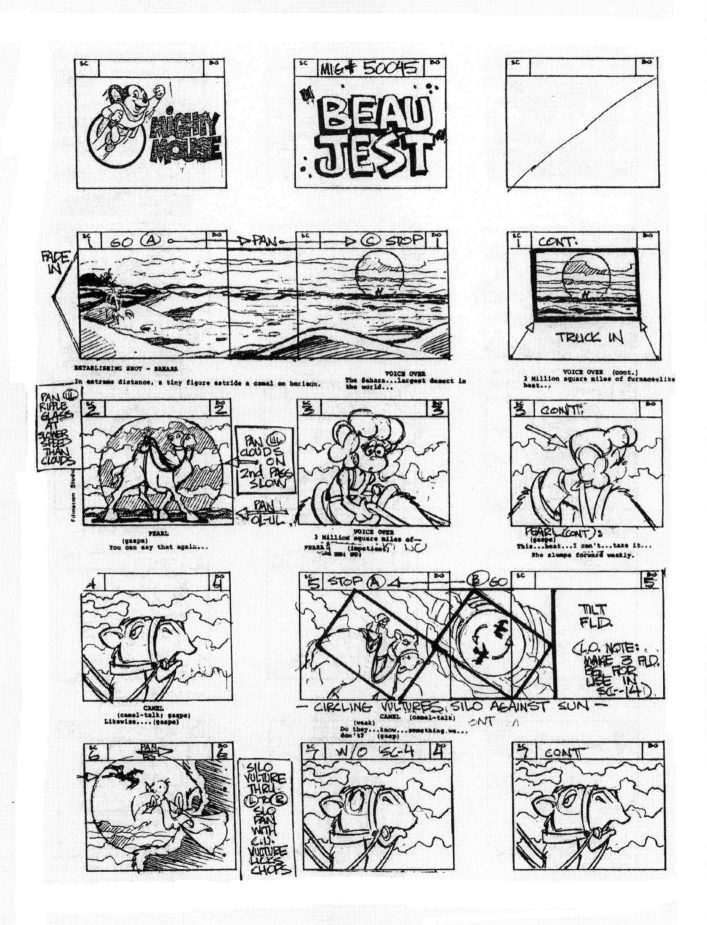

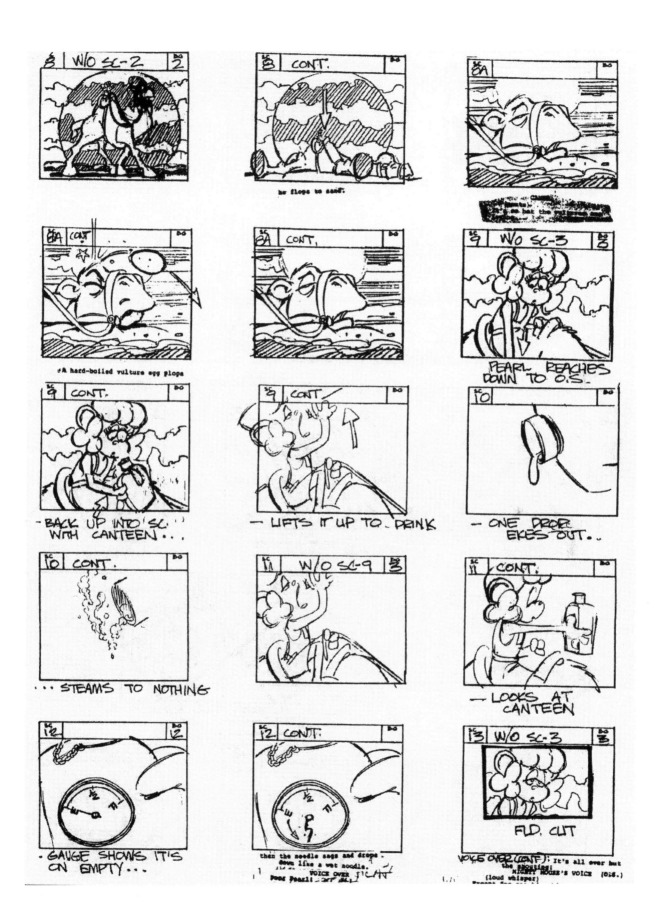

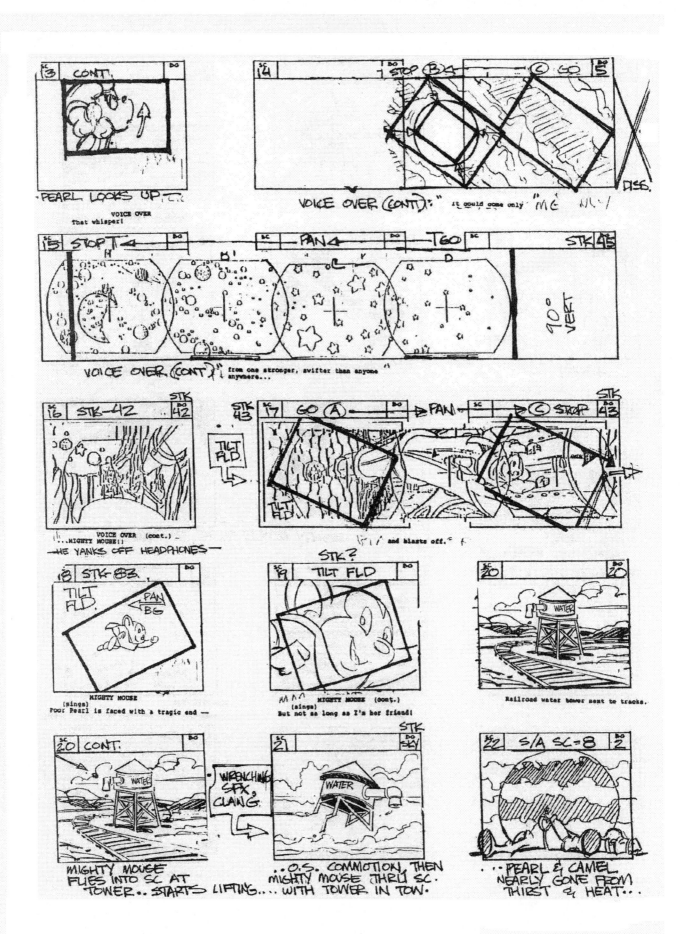

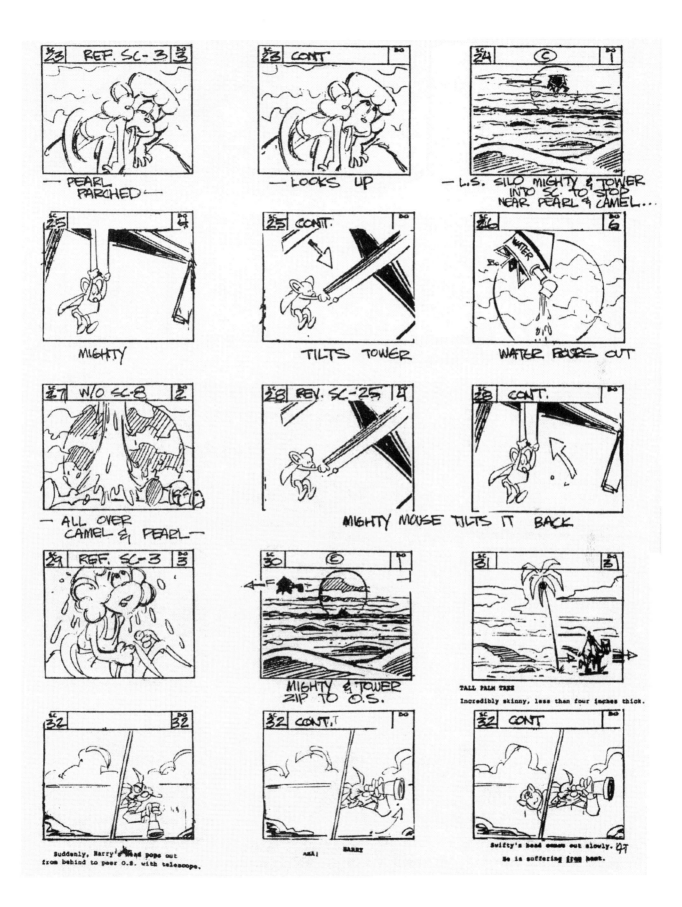

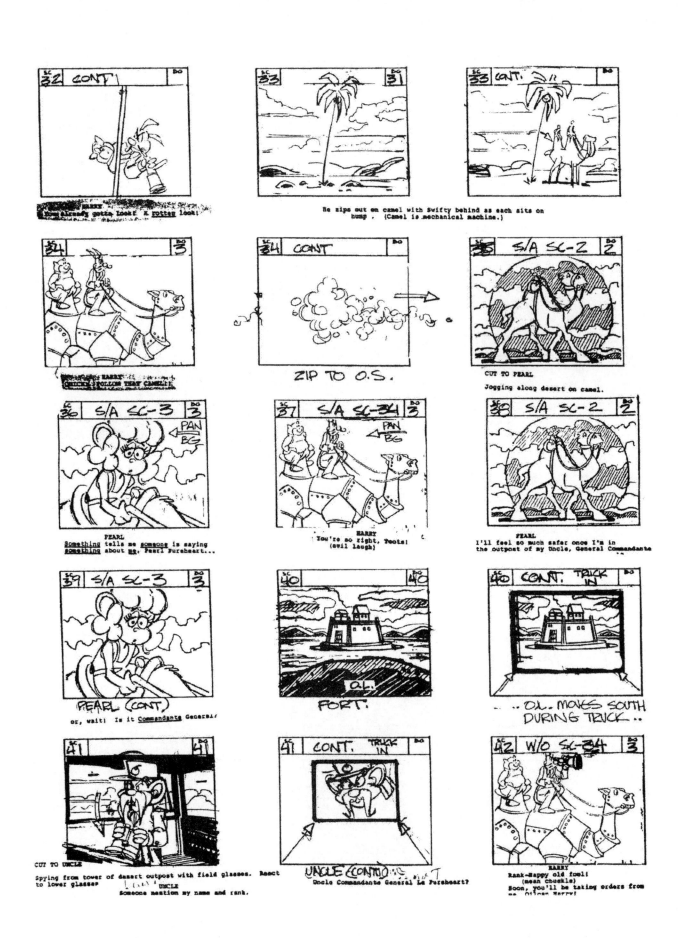

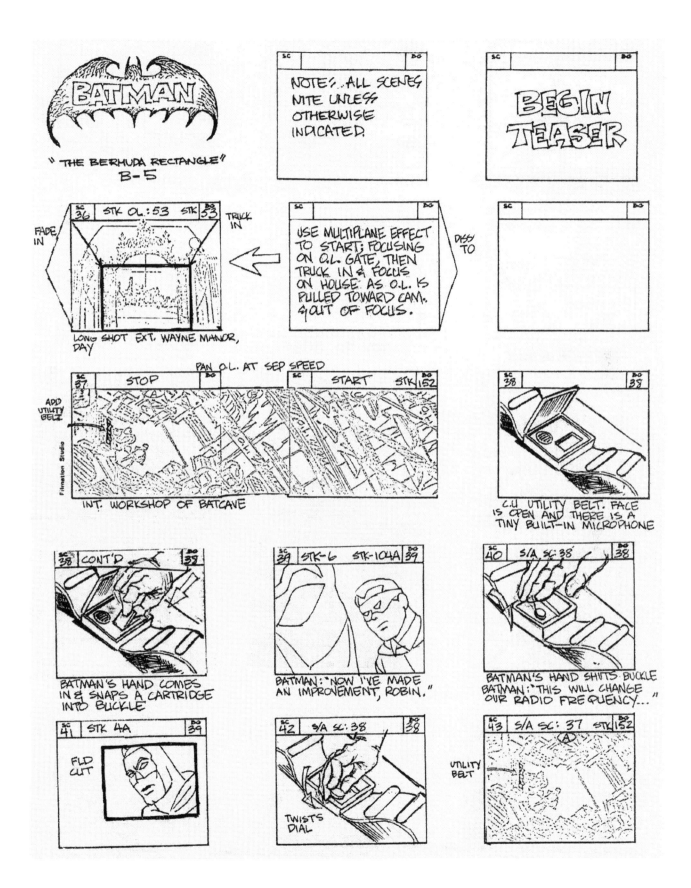

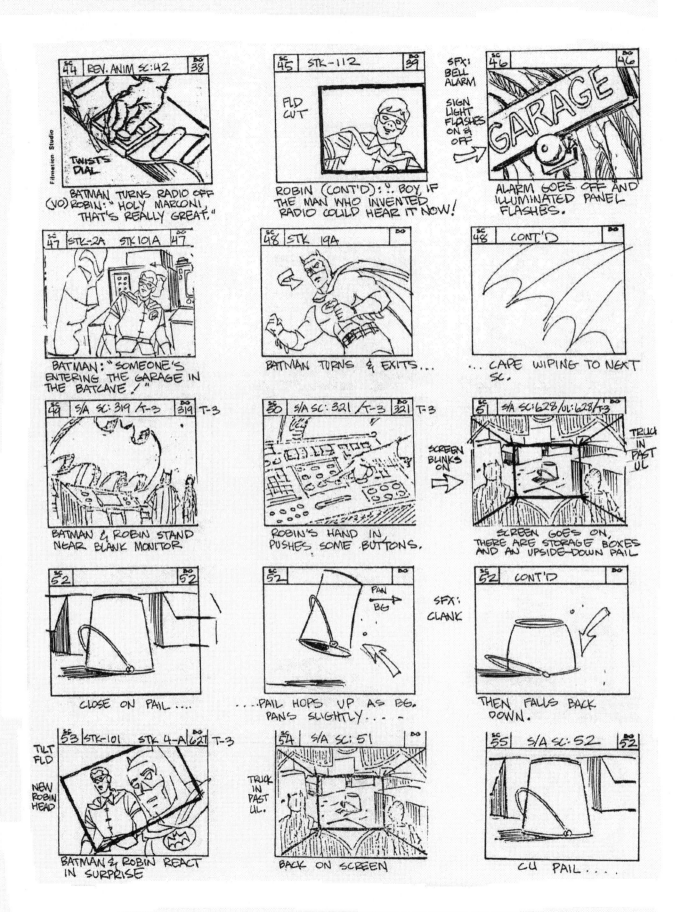

...PAIL HOPS UP THIS TIME LITTLE TINY FEETS POP OUT.....

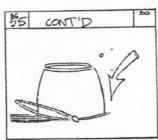
...AND CLANKS BACK DOWN

BATMAN SMILES
BATMAN: "MAYBE IT'S TIME."

(VO) ROBIN: "YOU MEAN LIKE 'KEEPING OFF..."

BATMAN: "EXACTLY!"

WIPE TO....

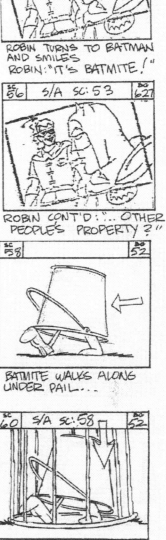

ROBIN TURNS TO BATMAN AND SMILES
ROBIN: "IT'S BATMITE!"

ROBIN CONT'D: "...OTHER PEOPLE'S PROPERTY?"

BATMITE WALKS ALONG UNDER PAIL...

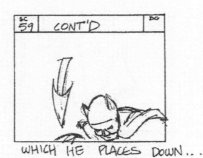
BATMAN HAS HEAVY BIRD CAGE WITH NO BOTTOM....

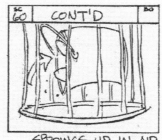
WHICH HE PLACES DOWN...

OVER PAIL & BATMITE.

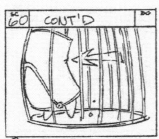
PAIL BUMPS

....SPROINGS UP IN AIR...

...CLANKS DOWN...

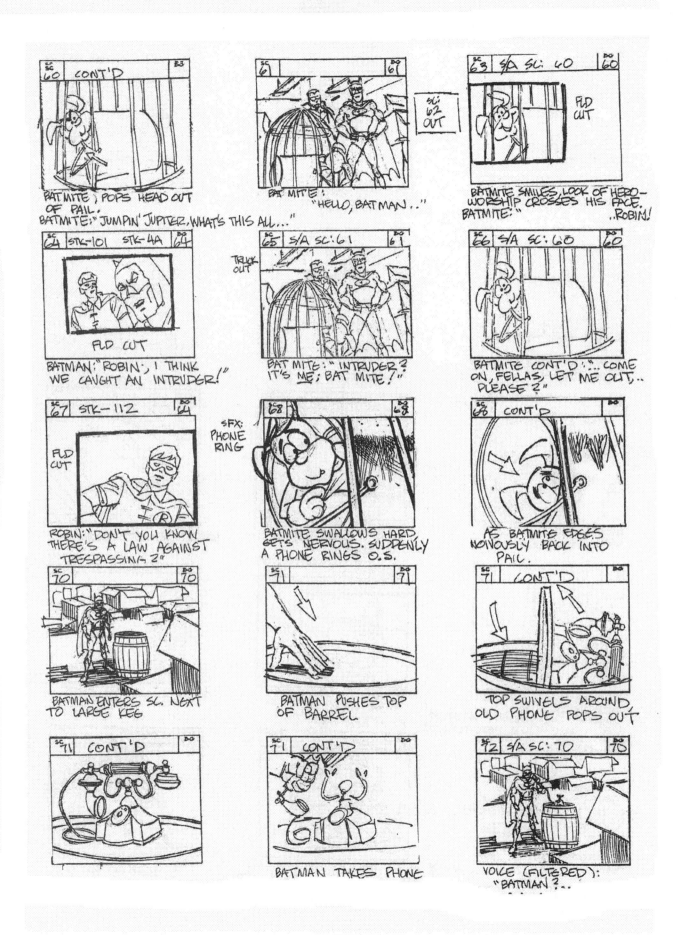

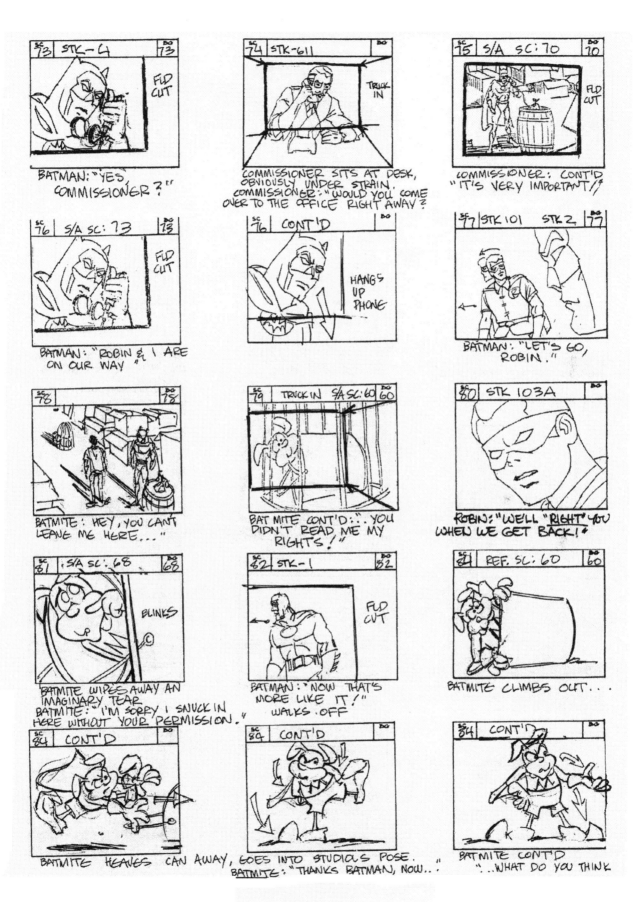

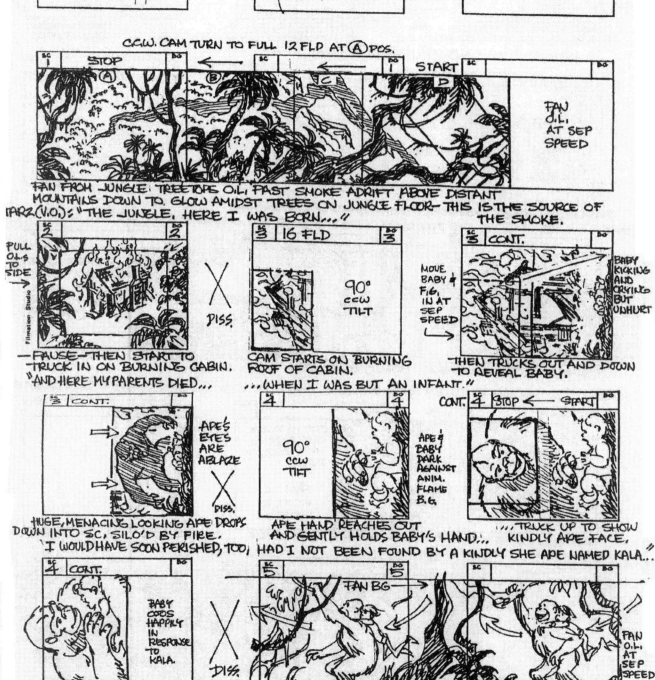

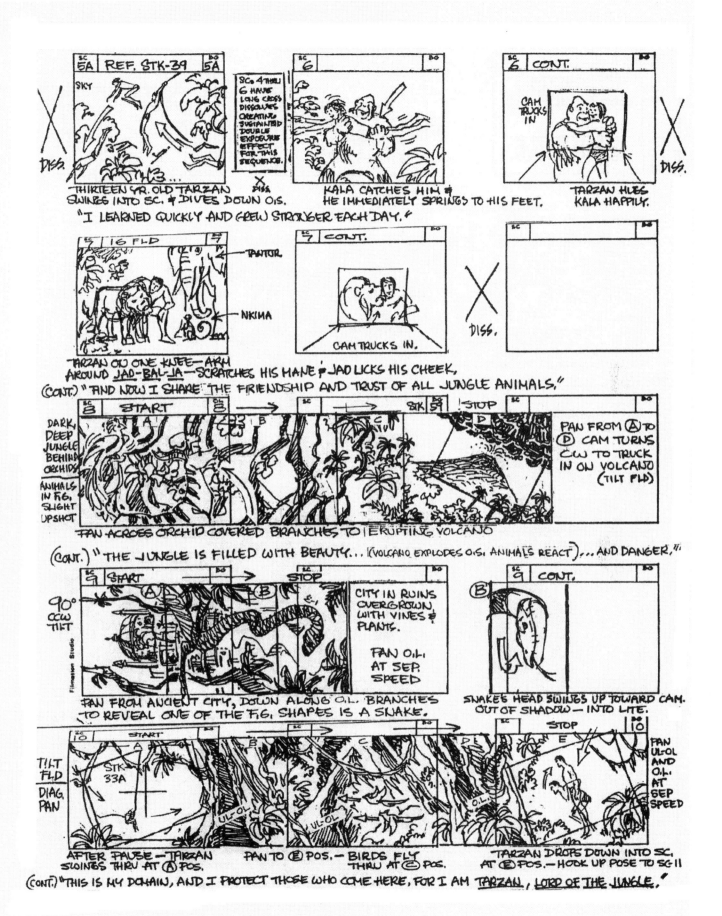

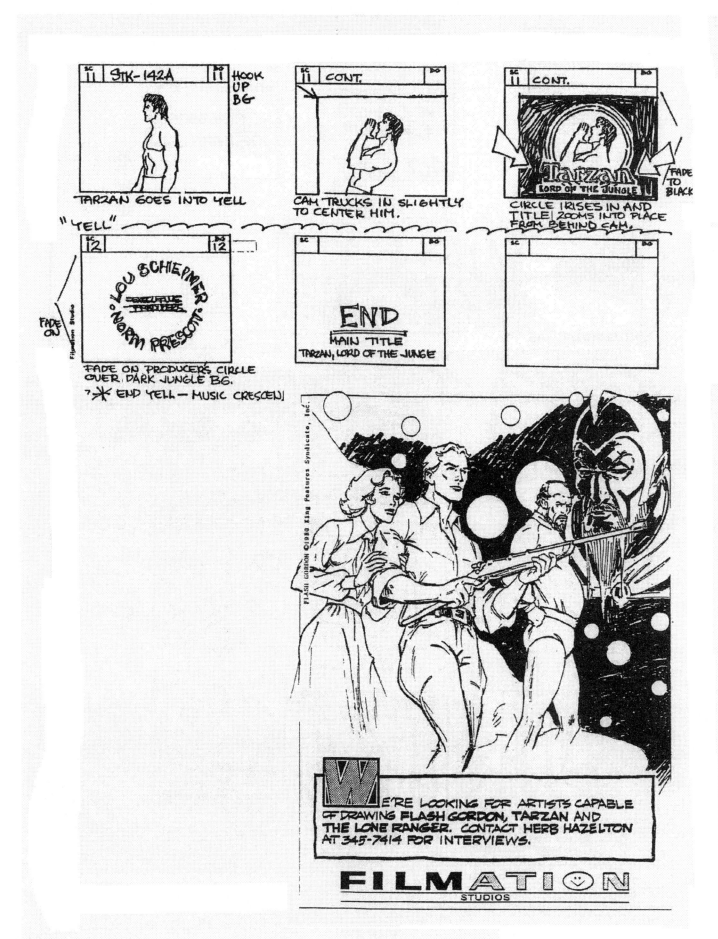

ANIMATED SERIES FOR TELEVISION

Alley Oop
Aquaman
Archies, The
Archie's Funhouse
Archies Specials
Archie's TV Funnies

Batman and Robin, The Adventures of
Brady Kids, The
Bravestarr
Broom Hilda
Brown Hornet, The
Blackstarr

Captain and the Kids, The

Dick Tracy

Emmy Lou

Fantastic Voyage
Fat Albert and the Cosby Kids
Fat Albert Specials
Flash, The
Flash Gordon, The New Adventures of
Fraidy Cat
Freedom Force, The

Gilligan, The New Adventures of
Great Space Race, The
Green Lantern
Ghost Busters
Groovie Goolies, The

Hardy Boys, The
Hawkman
Heckle and Jeckle
He-Man and the Masters of the Universe

Journey to the Center of the Earth

Kid Superpower Hour with Shazam!

Lassie and the Rescue Rangers
Lone Ranger, The

Manta and Moray
Mighty Mouse
Mission: Magic!
M. U. S. H.
My Favorite Martians

Sabrina, the Teenage Witch
Star Trek
Superboy
Superman, The New Adventures of
Superstretch and Microwoman

Tarzan, Lord of the Jungle
Tom and Jerry

Uncle Croc's Block

Wacky and Packy
Waldo Kitty
Web Woman

Young Sentinels

Zorro, The New Adventures of

FILMATION STUDIOS HISTORY OF SHOWS

1966-1967
The New Adventures of
Superman (with Superboy)

1967-1968
Aquaman / Superman Hour of Adventure
(with Guest Super Stars)
Journey to the Center of the Earth

1968-1969
The Archies
Batman / Superman Hour
Fantastic Voyage

1969-1970
Archie's Comedy hour, starring Sabrina, the Teenage Witch
The Hardy Boys
Sabrina, the Teenage Witch

1970-1971
Archie's Fun House
Will The Real Jerry Lewis Please Sit Down?
Sabrina and The Groovie Goolies

1971-1972
Archie's TV Funnies

1972-1973
Fat Albert and the Cosby Kids
The Brady Kids

1973-1974
Everything's Archie
My Favorite Martians
Mission Magic
Lassie's Rescue Rangers
Star Trek

1974-1975
U.S. of Archie
Shazam! (Live Action)
The New Adventures of Gilligan

1975-1976
Shazam-Isis Hour
Ghost Busters (Live Action)
Uncle Croc's Block
The Adventures of Waldo Kitty (originally called The Secret Lives of Waldo Kitty)

1976-1977
Tarzan, Lord of the Jungle
Ark II (Live Action)
Journey Back to Oz (Seen December 1976)
2 Hour Prime Time Special
The New Adventures of Batman

1977 - 1978
Space Sentinels
(originally called The Young Sentinels)
Space Academy (Live Action)
The Batman-Tarzan Adventure Hour
The Bang Shang Lalapalooza Show
(Starring Archie)
The Superwitch Show
(Starring Sabrina)
Fat Albert Halloween Special
Fat Albert Christmas Special "Silent Knights"

1978-1979
The Fabulous Funnies
Tarzan and the Super 7
Jason of Star Command (Live Action)
Space Academy (Live Action)

1979-1980
The New Adventures of Flash Gordon
Fat Albert and the Cosby Kids
(with the Brown Hornet)
The New Adventures of Mighty Mouse
Fat Albert Easter Special
Jason, of Star Command (Live Action)
A Snow White Christmas Special

1980-1981
The New Adventures of Tom and Jerry
(with Droopy)
Sport Billy (made for overseas)
Fat Albert "Follow the Leader" (nutritional spot to be shown in schools)
Fat Albert Department Of Energy Spot

(Subject: Conservation)

1981-1982
Tarzan, Lone Ranger, Zorro Adventure Hour
Blackstar
The Kid Super Power Hour
    (with: **Hero High, Shazam!** and
        Live Action Wrap-a-rounds)

1982-1983
Gilligan's Planet

1983-1985
He-Man and the Masters of the Universe

1985 - 1986
She-Ra, The Princess of Power

1986 - 1987
Ghost Busters (Animated)

1987 - 1988
Bravestarr
Bravestarr the Legend

Printed in Germany
by Amazon Distribution
GmbH, Leipzig